Guide to the places of the Etruscans

texts by *Maurizio Martinelli* and *Giulio Paolucci*
edited by *Claudio Strinati*

SCALA

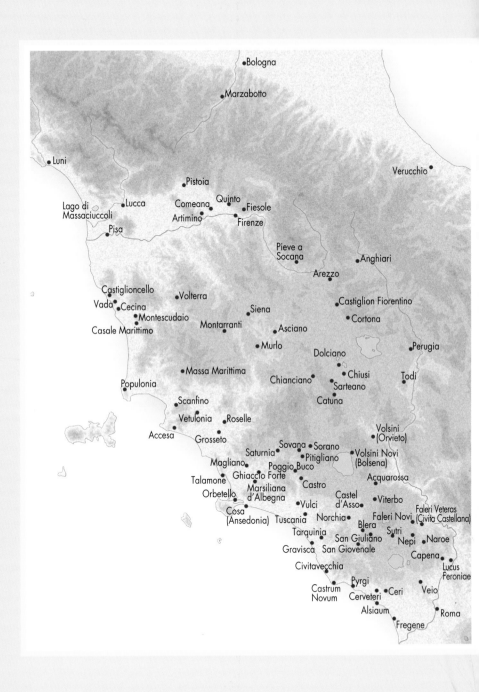

TABLE OF CONTENTS

Introduction

HISTORICAL BACKGROUND

The Etruscans established themselves in the area bounded by the Tiber to the south, the Arno to the north, the Apennine mountains to the east and the Tyrrhenian sea to the west, which took the name of Etruria from them, and also settled in Campania and the Po valley. At the beginning of the Iron Age, the Villanova culture was an organic part of Etruscan culture, and there was no central government, no uniform legislation or even well-established borders. From the earliest traces, Etruscan culture is distinct from the Greek, by which it was profoundly influenced, and from the Roman, which instead absorbed traditions and customs from the Etruscans. At the end of the eighth century BC, rich aristocracies began to emerge that would manifest their prosperity by constructing their monumental earth-covered tombs during the following century. This was the Orientalizing period, named for the strong influences that came from the eastern Mediterranean, documented by the importation of ceramics and metal objects, and the local italic imitations of the forms, the decorative syntax and the figurative repertory of that area. The wealth of Etruria also depended on the availability of mineral resources that fostered economic and cultural growth. At the end of the seventh century BC urban centers began to dominate the coastline, and quickly expanded to notable dimensions. This growth preceded the archaic period (end seventh – mid fifth centuries BC). The organization of city-states, led by an oligarchy of aristocrats, was also accompanied by the development of agriculture and mercantile activities. Ceramic workshops were built and they fabricated great quantities of pottery, including the characteristic black ware. During the sixth century BC, the political organization was based on twelve autonomous city-states (Veio, Cerveteri, Tarquinia, Vulci, Roselle, Vetulonia, Orvieto, Chiusi, Perugia, Cortona, Arezzo and Volterra) which met annually to honor their divinities with solemn sacrifices and participate in competitive games at the Voltumna shrine in Orvieto. Between the sixth and fifth centuries Etruscan sea power was expanding: after defeating the Focesi at Alalia in 535 BC, the Etruscans invaded Corsica. Shortly thereafter the situation changed radically with grave consequences for the history of Etruria. In 474 BC the southern coastal cities were gravely defeated by Hieron of Syracuse at Cuma. Threats also began to arrive from

The Banditaccia necropolis with burial mounds, Cerveteri.

beyond the Alps. At the beginning of the fourth century BC, Gallic tribes occupied areas of the Po valley and towns founded by the Etruscans, with the exception of Mantua, thus marking the end of Tyrrhenian domination of northern Italy. During the second half of the century, the Romans conquered Veio, Vulci and Volsinii. During the third century BC the rest of Etruria was overcome and the region was progressively absorbed into Roman culture.

LANGUAGE

The Etruscan language has been the subject of harsh debates and controversy, from the alphabet itself to the fact that they wrote from right to left. A Western Greek alphabet was already in use during the seventh century BC. However, although reading the words poses no particular problems, it is difficult to interpret the meaning because we have no equivalent of the Rosetta stone for the Etruscan language. Most of the known terms come from funerary and celebratory inscriptions. Noteworthy sources also include the *Tabula cortonensis*, containing 206 words related to judicial matters, and a bilingual text dated circa 500 BC, in Etruscan and Punic, on three gold sheets discovered in the Pyrgi sanctuary.

RELIGION

The religious expressions of the Etruscans evolved continuously. The animism focused on abstract principles or natural elements of the early Iron Age was replaced, as a result of Hellenistic influence from the seventh century forward, by a pantheon of anthropomorphic deities similar to the Greek gods. The most important of these were Tinia (Zeus), Uni (Hera) and Menrva (Athena). The Etruscan religion was based on rigid respect

Tabula cortonensis,
third-second centuries BC.
Museo della Città Etrusca
e Romana, Cortona.

Model of a temple.

of rituals and divination: from the observation of lightning, the flights of birds, the examination of the livers of sacrificed animals, priests attempted to interpret the will of the gods and to foresee the future. During the early Iron Age, the cult was practiced in the open or in huts; later it was housed in a dedicated space inside the palaces of the aristocracy, and in temples after the sixth century BC. The temple had a pronaos, or columned porch at the front, and was composed of three contiguous cells or a central room (*cella*) flanked by two narrow rooms that were open to the front (*alae*). The side walls were sometimes elongated to contain the columns (always in lines of even numbers) and this case were called *in antis*. A wooden architrave rested on the columns of the façade and was faced with painted terracotta panels. The longitudinal beams (*mutuli*) extended over this and the ends of the beams were also covered with decorated terracotta panels. Colorful terracotta ornaments covered all of the wooden elements of the roof; special tiles with heads or figures were aligned at the base of the roof. The cult of the deceased was of great importance. Cremation and burial were both practiced. In the case of cremation, the ashes were placed in a vase covered by a dish or a helmet, and then deposited, with the objects of the deceased, at the bottom of a cylindrical excavation in earth or rock. The little pit was closed with a slab of stone. For burials a rectangular grave was dug for the body of the deceased, accompanied by a series of personal objects. During the Orientalizing period underground tombs covered by mounds replaced these rites: the grave or the pit were too small to contain the elaborate

Detail of terracotta slab with banqueting scene from Acquarossa, sixth century BC. Museo Civico, Viterbo.

Impasto ossuary from Volterra, ninth-eighth centuries BC. Museo Etrusco Guarnacci, Volterra.

settings and belongings and to serve for several family members. Between the seventh and sixth centuries BC tombs were erected inside a low cylinder of stone or drum, above which a cone of earth was accumulated to protect the structures. A sloping hallway (*dromos*) led down to the underground chambers. Some of these tombs were completely excavated in rock, others were partially or completely constructed. Sometimes the architects of the tombs reproduced the whole plan of the aristocratic homes, with several rooms around a central atrium, decorated portals, seating and beds. Another type, that was widely used in southern Etruria where banks of tuff occur naturally in nature, was the cube tomb. These also aspired to recreate a sort of habitation and were constituted by a cubic construction, detached from the wall of rock, with a sculpted door which was often false, and a central burial chamber. Alternately aligned in several rows, the funerary complexes created very striking settings.

POTTERY AND OTHER PRODUCTIONS

Black vases, known as *bucchero* ceramics, are typical of Etruscan culture. The ceramists of Cerveteri, in their intent to imitate the appearance of metal vases, developed a specific firing technique to obtain uniformly black ceramics. The pottery was turned with clay which may have included additions of manganese or organic components, it was smoothed and decorated with incisions or pressed or applied designs while still crude and left to dry. The typical color was obtained in the firing: the kilns were closed so that the vases slowly carbonized in the oxygen-poor atmosphere. When the firing was finished, the pieces were polished while still hot. The development of the noble class favored the production of personal ornaments using various techniques: granulation, embossing and engraving. Pins and buckles of metal, which were used to fasten tunics and mantles, were sometimes decorated with figures in relief or other types of ornaments.

Bucchero jug with bull head. Museo Archeologico, Florence.

Bucchero *askos* in the shape of a charioteer from Caere, late seventh century BC. Museo Gregoriano Etrusco, Vatican.

Major Etruscan Cities in Latium

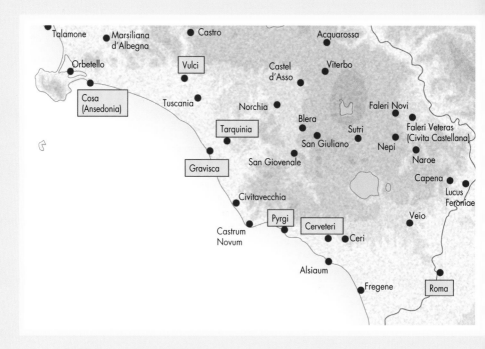

CAERE (CERVETERI)

Caere (Caisria in Etruscan) stood on a vast platform of tuff not far from the sea. It had been founded during the Villanova era, however its great economic, cultural and artistic flowering took place during the Orientalizing period (seventh century BC). This exceptional growth seems to have been the result of a flourishing maritime commercial activity, conducted chiefly through the ports of Alsium and Pyrgi. Today the necropolises laid out around the city conserve the memory of its importance in the past: the vast cemetery of Banditaccia to the north, the tombs of Monte Abatone to the south and those of Sorbo to the west, where the earliest tombs date back to the ninth-eighth centuries BC. The oldest tombs imitate the interior of huts, while the larger and more sumptuous ones are based on the dwellings of wealthy aristocrats, such as the Tomb of the Shields and Chairs in the tumulus of the same name. A dromos leads to a large vestibule adorned with large carved shields, mounted above a number of biers and two

chairs with high curved backs and footrests, set against the rear wall. From the vestibule three doors lead to three chambers with pitched roofs and biers aligned along the walls. The Tomb of the Capitals, instead, takes its name from a room adorned with octagonal columns and capitals that support a coffered ceiling. Another tomb of considerable interest is that of the Five Chairs, made up of two small chambers located at the sides of the access corridor. The wall of one of the chambers is lined with five chairs with footrests, where terracotta figurines must once have been seated. The Tomb of the Alcove is much later, circa fourth century BC, and has a different structure. The Tomb of the Reliefs is another example of fourth century Etruscan architecture. There are large burial niches with cushions set around the chamber, while the walls and the pillars are richly decorated with stucco representations of a large variety of objects that help to reconstruct the settings of everyday life and the furniture and utensils

Sections of the Banditaccia
Necropolis at Cerveteri.

used in the home. Some of the graves contain the remains of wall paintings, like the Tumulus of the Animal Paintings which covers four groups of chambers and takes its name from the tomb decorated with paintings, including an Orientalizing style figure of a lion. The necropolis of Monte Abatone has many tumuli, including the Campana Tomb (seventh century BC) with a carved ceiling and mock columns on the walls.

Interior of the tumulus of the Painted Animals, Banditaccia Necropolis.

Interior of the Tomb of the Capitals, late seventh century BC.

Bucchero vase in the form of a warrior's head from the Banditaccia Necropolis, Cerveteri, seventh century BC. Museo Nazionale Etrusco di Villa Giulia, Rome.

PYRGI

The most important of the ports on the Tyrrhenian coast constructed by Caere was Pyrgi, near Santa Severa. The sacred area was discovered a short distance from the sea and excavations have revealed the imposing foundation walls of two places of worship set side by side, built of large squared blocks. Temple B, dated to the end of the sixth century BC, has a single cell with a pronaos and columned peristyle. Temple A, datable to the middle of the fifth century BC, on a Tuscan plan with a colonnade at the front and three cells at the back, had a rich series of terracotta decorations, now in the *Museo di Villa Giulia* in Rome. The famous gold plaques with inscriptions (two in Etruscan and one in Phoenician) were also found in the sacred area. The bilingual text seems to point to close relations between the Etruscan city and Carthage.

Detail of clay group with mythological scene from the Theban cycle, from the area of temple A at Pyrgi, mid-fifth century BC. Museo Nazionale Etrusco di Villa Giulia, Rome.

Gold plaques with inscriptions in Etruscan and Phoenician, from sacred area C of Pyrgi, late sixth century BC. Museo Nazionale Etrusco di Villa Giulia, Rome.

TARQUINII (TARQUINIA)

Known as Tarquinii, Tarchuna or Tarchna to the Etruscans, substantial vestiges discovered in the Calvario and Monterozzi localities attest to the vitality of Tarquinia even in the Villanovan era. Villages of huts stood here that were then abandoned over the course of the eighth century BC, when the first nucleus of the Etruscan city was formed on the vast tufaceous plateau. The phenomenon of funerary painting had already begun to emerge in the early decades of the sixth century, with simple ornamental decorations executed on the walls of some tombs, as the upper classes began to draw attention to the social status they had achieved. Among the oldest and best-known examples, the tomb of the Bulls (circa 530 BC) which belonged to the important Spurinna family is particularly worthy of note. The tomb of the Augurs (circa 520 BC) has only one chamber, decorated on the back wall with two male figures, set on each side of a door. On the other walls there are scenes of games, A different atmosphere characterizes the Hunting and Fishing Tomb (circa 510 BC), where a young man about to dive from a rock is set in a lively landscape with birds in flight and darting fish. Similar themes are to be found in the tomb of the Hunter (510-500 BC), transformed into a spacious tent from which animals can be seen grazing, and in that of the Lionesses (520 BC), with figures of guests at a banquet lying on patches of grass and watching men and women dancing. One of the best-known painted tombs is undoubtedly that of the Leopards (480-470 BC), named after the figures of felines on the pediment of the rear wall, which has pairs of diners lying on *klinai* and entertained by musicians. The tombs were still built over the following decades, but the serene depictions of everyday life, profoundly imbued

Flautist entertaining the banqueters, Tomb of the Leopards, 480-470 BC.

Figures saying farewell at the sides of the door of the Afterlife, Tomb of the Augurs, 520 BC.

Following pages:
Scene with diver, Hunting and Fishing Tomb, 510 BC.

with realism, that had been their most evident feature gave way to darker visions, thronged with demons and scenes of the journey to the next world. The extraordinary Orcus Tomb dates from this period. At the beginning of the fourth century Tarquinii appears, in contrast with the trend in much of the rest of Etruria, to have been a thriving city, capable of controlling a vast territory and making its political weight felt in the "Etruscan confederation", i.e. "the league of twelve peoples". This economic growth also found expression in a revival of building activity and Tarquinii was fortified with walls about 5 miles long which followed the contours of the Civita hill and surrounded an area of about 320 acres. After military offensives against Rome (35? and 351 BC) failed, the city began to decline and, in 281 BC, Rome succeeded in conquering the great Etruscan city.

Detail of a banqueting
scene, Tomb of the
Leopards, 480-470 BC.

Detail of the face of Velia
Velcha in the Orcus Tomb,
third quarter of the fourth
century BC.

Head of Aita (Hades)
in the Orcus II Tomb, first
half of the fourth century
BC. Tarquinia.

THE MUSEO ARCHEOLOGICO NAZIONALE IN TARQUINIA

The prosperity attained by Tarquinii over the course of the 7th and 6th centuries is amply testified by the extensive collection of pottery, arranged by category since the original context of provenance is unknown. There are large numbers of vessels produced in Corinth and imitations made by local potters, in addition to those imported from Eastern Greece and, in particular, ointment jars of various forms. Representing animals and parts of the human body, such as legs and helmed heads, these must have held unguents of foreign manufacture. Also of great significance is the collection of *bucchero* vases, which includes a krater decorated by the Berlin Painter (500-490 BC) with an image of Europa and the bull. A large *amphora* representing the struggle between Apollo and Heracles for the tripod was executed by Pinthias (520-510 BC). The majestic terracotta winged horses dating from the beginning of the 4th cent. BC used to adorn the monumental sanctuary of the *Ara della Regina* (Altar of the Queen), which stood on the plateau of La Civita. Another particularly important personage in the Tarquinii of the first half of the 3rd century was Laris Pulena, interred in the *Sarcophagus of the magistrate*. The visit concludes with the reconstruction of several tombs with wall paintings (tomb of the Chariots, tomb of the *Triclinium*, tomb of the Ship, tomb of the Olympics) that were detached and moved to the museum, along with the Bruschi Tomb and the tomb of the Black Sow, which are not on display.

Rhyton made in Attica attributed to Charinos, from Tarquinii, early fifth century BC. Museo Archeologico Nazionale, Tarquinia.

Sarcophagus of the Magnate from the tomb of the Partunu, third quarter of the fourth century BC. Museo Archeologico Nazionale, Tarquinia.

Incense-burner cart from the Monterozzi Necropolis in Tarquinia, first quarter of the eighth century BC. Museo Archeologico Nazionale, Tarquinia.

The *Winged Horses* from the sanctuary of the *Ara della Regina* in Tarquinia, early fourth century BC. Museo Archeologico Nazionale, Tarquinia.

Following pages: *Sarcophagus of the Magistrate* from Tarquinii, late third - early second centuries BC. Museo Archeologico Nazionale, Tarquinia.

GRAVISCA (PORTO CLEMENTINO)

The old port of Tarquinii, was founded at the beginning of the sixth century BC, south of the mouth of the Marta river, on what would later be the site of the Roman colony of Gravisca. Greater information has come from the excavation of the Archaic sanctuary, which, on the basis of the dedications in Etruscan and Greek, appears to have been consecrated to Turan-Aphrodite. Other deities were venerated there that can be identified with the Greek goddesses Demeter (Vei in Etruscan) and Hera (Uni in Etruscan). Herodotus praised the sanctuary and the fabulous wealth accumulated through trade.

VULCI

The ancient city of Vulci, called Velch by the Etruscans, stood in a naturally protected position on a large plateau just over 7 miles from the coast. The important Etruscan settlement was located at the center of a fertile region extending between the Fiora and the Albegna valleys. Numerous necropolises (with well, pit and chest tombs) from the Iron Age have been found around the Vulci plateau and seem to suggest a series of separate villages. Objects of foreign origin were already present among the grave goods in this period, demonstrating the existence of extensive trade relations. These include the bronze figure of a warrior imported from Sardinia (second half of the ninth century BC) that has given the tomb of the Nuraghic Bronze its name. the most interesting of which is the Euboean krater found at Pescia Romana and now in the Grosseto Museum. The tomb of the Bronze Chariot, dated to 680-670 BC, constitutes a record of extraordinary importance owing to its rich contents, relating to the custom of the banquet, which accompanied

Euboean krater by the Cesnola Painter, from Pescia Romana, 730-720 BC. Museo Archeologico e d'Arte della Maremma, Grosseto.

Above: Stone anchor with inscription dedicated to Aeginetan Apollo by Sostratus, from Gravisca, late sixth century BC. Museo Archeologico Nazionale, Tarquinia and Youth astride a sea monster from the necropolis of Poggio Maremma, Vulci, mid-sixth century BC. Museo Nazionale Etrusco di Villa Giulia, Rome.

COSA (ANSEDONIA)

Cosa was constructed by the Romans in 273 BC. The city stood in an elevated position on a sheer promontory above the sea, and occupied an area of about 32 acres. The forum housed the city's public buildings (*curia, comitia, basilica*). The sacred buildings were located in the highest part of the city, the acropolis (arx), defended by its own ring of walls with two gates. The majestic remains of the Capitolium (150 BC) dedicated to Jupiter-Juno-Minerva, built on the site of a previous place of worship, are to be found in this area. It had a sumptuous decoration of terracotta slabs that are now on display in the local museum, The city was connected with its port (Portus Cosanus), of which some imposing structures have survived, along with the so-called Tagliata or "Cut," a canal about 330 feet long that runs partly in the open and partly through a tunnel to provide a link between the open sea and the lagoon.

at least three burials, and the bronze chariot with embossed decorations from which it takes its name. Later graves continue to reflect the thriving state of Vulci's economy for the rest of the seventh century, as the rich materials from the tomb of Isis in the necropolis of La Polledrara clearly indicate: terracotta statuettes of women, flasks, Egyptian scarabs and ostrich eggs with a lavish ornamentation that can be attributed to the sophisticated local craftsmen, like the numerous bronze artifacts found in the same complex. In the final decades of the century there was also a prolific production of pottery based on Greek models, which was accompanied by a series of sculptures in nenfro (volcanic rock), many of them representing fantastic animals like the well-known statues of a centaur and of a youth astride a sea monster, both in the Museo di Villa Giulia.

Centauro in nenfro. Museo Nazionale Etrusco di Villa Giulia, Rome.

Statue of a woman from the Tomb at La Polledrara, Vulci, 570-560 BC. British Museum, London.

View of the remains of the *Capitolium* on the acropolis of Cosa.

THE MUSEO NAZIONALE ETRUSCO DI VILLA GIULIA

Five rooms of the museum are devoted to the city of Vulci. They include bronze statuettes of Sardinian production (among them a small figure with a tall headdress and large shield). Other materials from the Villanovan period come from the cemeteries of the Osteria, including the extraordinary objects from the tomb of the Bronze Chariot (680-670 BC) comes from the cemeteries of the Osteria. The ancient city Bisentium or Visentium (modern Bisenzio), and especially the necropolis of Olmo Bello, has yielded grave goods of extraordinary interest: a ceremonial cart from the second half of the 8th century, adorned with various groups of statuettes and an amphora made of bronze plate, datable to 730-700 BC, the lid of which is decorated with seven figures dancing around a monstrous creature that can be identified as a god of the underworld. The rooms devoted to Veii contain the famous statues that used to stand on the roof of the sanctuary at Portonaccio, representing the contest between *Apollo and Heracles for Possession of the Ceryneian Hind* with its golden horns. Watching the hero engaged in his labor are *Leto Holding the Baby Apollo* and *Hermes*, masterpieces of Etruscan ceramics of the late

Head of Hermes from the sanctuary of Portonaccio at Veio, late sixth century BC. Museo Nazionale Etrusco di Villa Giulia, Rome.

Cinerary urn in bronze plate with scene of ritual dance, late eighth century BC. from the necropolis of *Olmo Bello* at Bisenzio. Museo Nazionale Etrusco di Villa Giulia, Rome.

th cent. BC. A reconstruction of the Maroi Tomb, discovered in the cemetery of the Banditaccia, introduces the vast collection of objects from Caere. Some of the oldest finds, datable to between the ninth and eighth centuries BC, come from the necropolises of the Cava della Pozzolana and Sorbo, but it is the celebrated *Sarcophagus of the Married Couple* (sixth century BC) from the Banditaccia that rivets attention. The famous bust of *Apollo*, that was once part of the great right relief on the pediment, dating from the late fourth-early third centuries BC, comes from the sanctuary discovered at the locality of Lo Scasato.

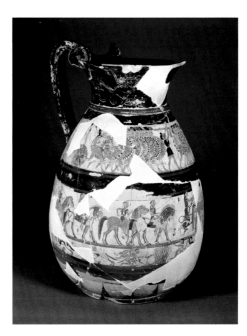

Olpe Chigi from Veio, second half of the seventh century BC. Museo Nazionale Etrusco di Villa Giulia, Rome.

Apollo di Scasato, second half of the fourth century BC. Museo Nazionale Etrusco di Villa Giulia, Rome.

Following pages: *Sarcophagus of the Married Couple* from the Banditaccia Necropolis at Cerveteri, a detail, second half of the sixth century BC. Museo Nazionale Etrusco di Villa Giulia, Rome.

The Upper Valley of the Tiber, *Veii* and the Lake of Bolsena

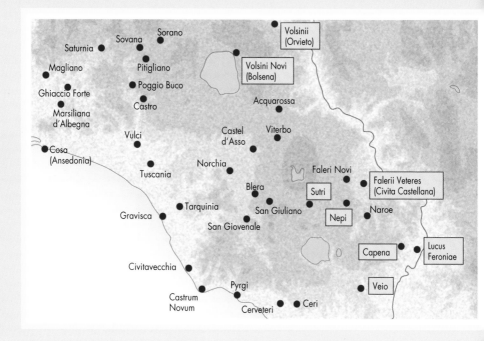

HE FALISCAN REGION, APENA AND LUCUS FERONIAE

he territory situated on the right bank of
e Tiber, bordered by lake Bracciano, the
abatini mountains, lake Vico and the Cimini
ountains, was occupied in the Iron Age by
e Falisci, a people of Italic stock who came
form a sort of buffer between the Etruscans,
e Sabines and the peoples of the Adriatic
gion. The most important Faliscan centers
cluded Falerii, Narce and Capena. The oldest
aces in Capena indicate that it was initially
e dominant Faliscan center, surrounded
y minor satellites. The burial finds of the
ghth and seventh centuries reflect a growing
rosperity throughout the area, accompanied
y a shift from well tombs for cremations to
t tombs for inhumations. These in turn gave
ay to chamber tombs, which soon became, at
Iarce for instance, the most common.
he intermediary role played by the Faliscan
rritory is confirmed by the stylistic influences
at were conveyed by the materials that
rived, through Veii, from Campania and
outhern Latium.
he presence of the sanctuary of Feronia in
Capena should also be interpreted in this
nse. It was already flourishing in the sixth
ntury BC. Located at the intersection of

main routes, it was sacked by Hannibal in 211
BC and then reconstructed. All that remains
now are the vestiges of walls and an altar in
the area of the Roman forum. It was originally
the location of the college of the priests called
hirpi (wolves), who carried out ceremonies
in the nearby sacred grove, including the rite
of walking on burning coals. In addition,
Feronia's role as the protectress of slaves made
the sanctuary the theater of ceremonies of
manumission and emancipation, i.e. formal
liberation from slavery. Enlarged in the Roman
era and abandoned in the Middle Ages, it is
now open to the public, along with the many
structures that have been brought to light,
including baths fed by the Aqua Augusta
aqueduct and the remains of places of worship.

Impasto *kantharos* from the
necropolis of San Martino
at Capena, second half
of the seventh century BC.
Museo Nazionale Etrusco
di Villa Giulia, Rome.

Lebes on openwork foot,
from the Pizzo Piede
necropolis at Narce, first half
of the seventh century BC.
Museo Nazionale Etrusco
di Villa Giulia, Rome.

FALERII (CIVITA CASTELLANA)

The growth of this city at the beginning of the fifth century is documented by a complicated urban renovation plan that gave prominence to the places of worship in the area of the settlement and its immediate surroundings. In addition to the temple on Vignale (fifth century BC), the sacred complex of Lo Scasato was laid out in the zone to the east of the plateau. Brought to light in 1886-87, it comprised a large square basin, about 43 feet on each side and over 26 feet deep, excavated in the rock and equipped with two flights of steps. The temple itself had a podium of blocks of tuff with a front almost 56 feet wide, facing west. Numerous pieces of terracotta facing, such as acroteria with palmettes and slabs carved in relief, were found on the site, as well as fragments of statues from the pediment. Some of the finds from this temple are now on display in the *Museo Archeologico dell'Agro Falisco* at Civita Castellana, while the rest can be seen at the Museo di Villa Giulia in Rome. The city was destroyed in 241 BC after a popular rebellion, when the Romans massacred 15,000 Faliscans. Later it was rebuilt on a different site, and was named, appropriately, *Falerii Novi*.

Tuff container with cinerary urn from *Falerii Veteres*, eighth century BC. Museo Nazionale Etrusco di Villa Giulia, Rome.

Terracotta head of a man from the temple of Lo Scasato at *Falerii*, first half of the fourth century BC. Museo Nazionale Etrusco di Villa Giulia, Rome.

Right: Olla on stand from the necropolis of Le Macchie at Civita Castellana, second half of the seventh century BC. Museo Archeologico dell'Agro Falisco, Civita Castellana.

SUTRI AND NEPI

Sutri, located on a spur of tuff isolated by the Promonte and Rotoli rivers, stood at the center of an area occupied from prehistoric times and during the Early Iron Age. The center served as a point of control over the corridor between the Cimini Mountains to the north and the Sabatini Mountains to the south, with their impenetrable forests, and provided the coastal cities, especially Caere, with a commercial outlet close to the Faliscan area, as well as a junction on the road from Nepi to Veii. It was after the fall of Veii in 396 BC that Sutri entered the Roman sphere of influence, becoming a center of strategic control, at the expense of the Falisci and the territories of Tarquinii. This is evident from the remains

we see today, all from the Roman era, such as the sections of the walls on the southwest and northeast sides, the Mithraeum converted into the church of the Madonna del Parto during the Middle Ages, a small complex of baths near the ancient forum and the amphitheater excavated in the tuff, capable of holding 3000-4000 spectators. The Etruscan rock tombs from pre-Roman Sutri remain: their contents are in the local *Museo del Patrimonium*. Nearby Nepi (Nepet to the Etruscans), whose cemeteries stretch back to the seventh century BC, was an important center of trade in the Archaic era, a role that is reflected in the Attic pottery found in graves and in the roads that linked it to Sutri and Veii. It was eventually absorbed by the Romans who founded a new colony for its control (383 or 373 BC).

View of the amphitheater at Sutri.

Front of the rock necropolis at Sutri.

VEII (VEIO)

Veii (Veis to the Etruscans, Veio in modern Italian) stood on the right bank of the Tiber on a vast plateau bordered by the Cremera (now Valchetta) and Piordo rivers. The locality appears to have been inhabited since the Bronze Age, but it was only in the Iron Age that vast cemeteries, with well tombs in the oldest phase and pit tombs in the following period (eighth century BC), lined the main roads that linked the settlement of Veii to satellite centers in the area. In the Oriental period these gave way to pit burials with loculi to hold the grave goods and the chamber tomb made its appearance. One of these, at Riserva del Bagno (second quarter of seventh century BC), was painted with figures of ducks. Another rare tomb found in the necropolis of Monte Michele (called the Campana Tomb after its discoverer) and painted with figures of real and imaginary animals and people riding horses that are now hard to decipher, dates from later still (end of seventh century BC). A princely tomb has recently been excavated at the same locality, and its rich contents, along with other evidence, like the burial mounds at Vacchereccia and Monte Aguzzo, where the celebrated Chigi Olpe of Corinthian manufacture (Museo di Villa Giulia) was found, bear witness to the remarkable flourishing of the city in the Orientalizing period. During the sixth century Veii was given a truly urban layout. At Campetti there was a temple dedicated to a goddess of the underworld with the same name as the city, Veis, the equivalent of the Latin Ceres, and the great sanctuary of Iuno Regina, the city's guardian deity, stood near Piazza d'Armi which has now been excavated.

But the best known of the sanctuaries lay outside the walls, on a cliff above the Mola River at Portonaccio.

Apollo of Veii from the sanctuary of Portonaccio at Veio, late sixth century BC. Museo Nazionale Etrusco di Villa Giulia, Rome.

Opposite: *Statue of Latona and the young Apollo,* from the sanctuary of Portonaccio at Veio. Museo Nazionale Etrusco di Villa Giulia, Rome.

Interior of the Tomb of the Ducks, second quarter of the seventh century BC.

BISENZIO

This zone was already extensively occupied in the Early Iron Age, as the Villanovan finds made at Orvieto as well as at Bolsena-Gran Carro and Bisenzio indicate. The local culture, whose aspects are reflected in the grave goods of the Villanovan phase, is characterized by the rarity of biconical cinerary urns and the prevalence of hut urns instead, along with the richness of plastic decorations. While some pieces of particular significance are already known for the pre-Etruscan era, such as the hut urn from Olmo Bello, it was between the eighth and seventh centuries BC that the center displayed signs of a sudden increase in prosperity, especially with regard to bronze artifacts. The presence of small figures cast from solid bronze and applied as ornaments to cinerary urns, carts and amphorae, made out of embossed plate was typical of the local production. While the prototypes for this method of decoration were Oriental products, the choice of the themes depicted and the predilection for crowded

Incense-burner cart, second half of the eighth century BC. from the necropolis of Olmo Bello at Bisenzio. Museo Nazionale Etrusco di Villa Giulia, Rome.

Cinerary hut urn in bronz plate, from Vulci, mid-eighth century BC. Museo Nazionale Etrusco di Villa Giulia, Rome.

cenes in which spectacular effect and narrative content were preferred over refinement of detail appears totally autonomous and local in origin. One of the most significant examples is the incense-burner cart, used in religious ceremonies, found in Tomb II at Olmo Bello and dated to the second half of the eighth century. The crosspieces linking the wheels to the support of the receptacle are thronged with figures of warriors, women carrying amphorae on their heads, a plowman with a pair of oxen and a hunter with an animal on leash; in other words scenes of daily life and activities characteristic of members of society whose status was growing at the time. Equally important is the amphora made of bronze plate (late eighth century BC) from Tomb XII at Olmo Bello, whose shoulder and lid are decorated with two circular scenes, perhaps to be interpreted as moments in a religious ceremony connected with hunting or war.

THE AREA AROUND *VOLSINII*

What is now the headland of Gran Carro, on Lake Bolsena, was originally just one segment of the territory occupied by a village in the Early Iron Age. Underwater investigations have identified the remains of numerous lake dwellings, whose piles have been preserved in the mire. Taken altogether, the underwater finds in this lake of volcanic origin, already numerous for the middle of the II millennium BC, have made it possible to measure the increase in the water level with precision. Among the various discoveries from the Villanovan era, that of the Gran Carro is the most significant. The settlement was originally protected to the east by a rocky overhang and to the north by an elevation, as well as by a large dry-stone structure in the form of a truncated cone that was about 10 feet high and had an elliptical base measuring over 164 x 230 feet, on which an open space of about 115 x 180 feet was laid out. Along with spindles, mallets, chisels, fibulae and bits, the finds have included biconical vases for water or foodstuffs, cup-pails with tall handles, jars, jugs, mugs, bowls and ceramic cooking stoves in the form of a truncated cone. A distinctive feature is the presence of rounded vases with several spouts, perhaps used as oil lamps with several wicks. A short distance away, a 30-foot long dugout made from a single tree trunk has been identified on the lake bed.

Detail of the wall decoration of the Golini I Tomb, second half of the fourth century BC. Museo Archeologico Nazionale, Orvieto.

Following pages: a view of the necropolis of Crocefisso del Tufo.

Early Iron-Age crockery from the lake settlement of the Gran Carro in Bolsena Lake. Museo Civico Rocca Monaldeschi, Bolsena.

VOLSINII (ORVIETO)

Volsinii, or Velzna in Etruscan, from which modern name of Orvieto derives, was built atop a steep tuff crag. Materials from the Villanovan phase have been discovered. During the course of the seventh century BC, however, there are clear signs of growth, to be attributed not just to the agricultural potential of the area, but also to the settlement's strategic position at the confluence of the Paglia and Tiber rivers. The oldest part of the necropolis of the Cannicella, located on the southern side, where the

chamber tombs with pitched roofs are set on terraces, dates from the Orientalizing phase of Volsinii. Their contents include fine bucchero ware, examples of a local production that has been widely studied and is characterized by a sober decoration enriched with bands of figures, made by rolling cylinders with the design cut into them over the clay while still soft. Unusually, the lowest part of the cemetery housed a sanctuary from the last quarter of the sixth century devoted to funerary and fertility cults. The only covered space was adjacent to this. The materials unearthed here include the famous statue of Greek marble known as the Cannicella Venus, now on display at the Museo Faina. The other large burial ground, to the northwest of the city, is the necropolis of Crocefisso del Tufo, laid out during the sixth century according to a systematic plan like a city. The contents of the tombs at Crocefisso del Tufo, which include imported Attic pottery, attest to the affluence of the local families in the sixth and fifth centuries, and to the high artistic level attained by the local potters and metal workers. No residential districts have come to light, but numerous places of worship have been found in various parts of the city, of which the best-known and most legible is the temple of the Belvedere. It stood on a podium that was, in part, hewn out of the solid rock, and in part constructed, with a ramp or flight of steps that provided access. The pronaos in front, with one side at a slight angle, had two rows of four columns, with a three foot diameter, that stood in front of the three cells. Overall,

Venus, sculpture in Greek marble from the sanctuary of the Cannicella Necropolis, 530-520 BC. Museo Claudio Faina, Orvieto.

Above: Foundations of the Belvedere Temple, fifth century BC.

the plan has exactly the same proportions as those cited by architect Vitruvius, in his *De Architectura* treatise, for the Tuscan style of temple, typical of the Etruscans. The oldest facing materials of the building date from the beginning of the fifth century BC, while the majority of the pedimental sculptures are from the fifth-sixth centuries and come from the pediment at the rear. The sanctuary called Fanum Voltumnae, dedicated to Voltumna, an Archaic Etruscan deity who personified the principle of transformation and change in nature and life, was even better known in the literary tradition. At the time of the first conflicts with Rome, Volsinii seems to have seen a shift in the focus of its economic activities, hitherto characterized by the production of painted ware and silver-plated pottery, toward the farming of the territory. Many groups of graves were present in the territory, for instance at Settecamini, where chamber tombs were excavated in the tuff, including the two well-known Golini Tombs: the first (Golini I), preceded by a sloping passageway that led down to the quadrangular chamber with a short central screen; slightly more recent (second half of the fourth century), Golini Tomb II also had a single chamber and was decorated. The nearby tomb of the Warrior was roughly contemporary, and its rich contents included a dinner service (two situlae, a jug and a low decorated cup) accompanied by a complete set of bronze armor. While the neighboring rural centers prospered Volsinii, because it dominated the lines of communication, found itself caught up in a struggle with Rome. Clashes took place between the two cities in 392, in 308 (with the defeat at Lake Vadimone) and again in 294, 285 and 280 BC.

Terracotta *Heracles* from the Belvedere Temple, late fifth-early fourth century BC. Museo Archeologico Nazionale, Orvieto.

Wall with biga in the tomb of the Hescanas, near Porano, late fourth-early third centuries BC.

THE MUSEO ARCHEOLOGICO NAZIONALE IN ORVIETO

The Archeological Museum contains the materials formerly in the collection of the Cathedral Vestry Board, along with finds made in more recent excavations carried out in several sanctuaries in the city and in the surrounding burial grounds. The paintings from the Golini I and Golini II tombs, named for the man who discovered them, are on display in the museum and there is a substantial collection of architectural terracottas which adorned the many sanctuaries in Etruscan Orvieto, among them the remains of the decorative pediment of the Belvedere Temple, datable to between the end of the 5th and the early 4th century.

Opposite: Mirror with winged figure from the necropolis of Porano. Museo Archeologico Nazionale, Orvieto.

Kernos with faces of women from the necropolis of Settecamini. Museo Archeologico Nazionale, Orvieto.

MUSEO ARCHEOLOGICO "CLAUDIO FAINA"

The two-storey museum houses a collection of a national significance; the objects are presented by categories. Particular importance in the layout of the museum is assigned to Attic blackfigure pottery (represented by three large *amphorae* by Exekias, one of the greatest vase painters of the second half of the 6th cent. BC), red-figure pottery and the collection of Etruscan figurative ceramics. Among the latter it is worth singling out the vessels belonging to the so-called "Vanth group", after the name of the Etruscan divinity who accompanied the deceased into the underworld.

Vases called from the *Group of Vanth*, late fourth century BC. Museo Archeologico Claudio Faina, Orvieto.

Head of sarcophagus representing Ulysses and Circe, from Torre San Severo, late fourth century BC. Museo Archeologico Claudio Faina, Orvieto.

OLSENA

Archeological investigation has shown that Bolsena was not occupied until the third century BC. Its walls in *opus quadratum*, which stretched for almost 3 miles, are among its oldest structures. Letters of the Etruscan alphabet can still be seen on the ramparts of the castle. Several chamber tombs at Poggio Pesce Bolsena also date from that initial period in the city's history. It was given a strong boost in the second century BC with the opening of the Via Cassia, which passed through the city. This resulted in a substantial modification of the urban layout, which was divided up again into blocks by cross streets, although the more hilly areas maintained a high density of population, as the atrium houses of Poggio Moscini datable to just this phase demonstrate. The numerous workshops in the archeological area were constructed during the republican period, while the aqueduct, the baths with their cryptoporticus (calidarium and cistern) date to the first century AD. The remains of these buildings are currently open to the public.

Clay throne with panthers from Bolsena, second century BC. Museo Civico Rocca Monaldeschi, Bolsena.

Remains of walls with engraved Etruscan letters.

Rupestrian Etruria

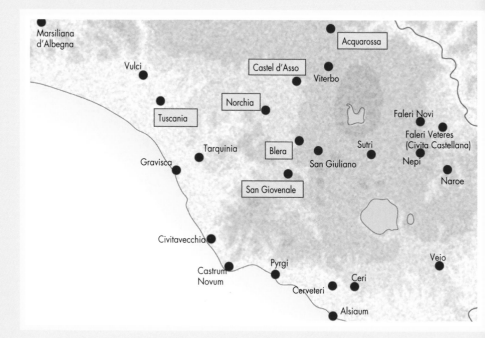

SAN GIOVENALE

San Giovenale stood on a plateau of considerable strategic significance for the control of the upper valley of the Mignone river.

A few Etruscan dwellings have been found: quadrangular in plan, they consisted of two rooms with foundations constructed of blocks of tuff and walls of unfired brick.

The cemeteries were laid out around the hill of San Giovenale and contain well, box and tumulus tombs, as well as those excavated in the rock.

Structures of the Etruscan settlement.

BLERA

The ancient town occupied part of a narrow shelf of tuff naturally defended by steep, high walls. Only a few remains of the settlement have come to light, chiefly sections of its massive walls, while those of the large necropolises that extended along the valleys of the Ricanale and Biedano are much more substantial. There is an evocative group of rock-cut tombs on the slope of Pian del Vescovo.

Several burial mounds can be dated to the oldest phase (seventh century BC), but the numerous cube and half-cube tombs of the sixth-fifth centuries BC are the most impressive sight. They have sculpted façades that, in some cases, reveal the structure of the pitched roof and the door leading to the mortuary chambers. The latter have platforms set against the walls or funeral beds arranged like Roman dining couches. A tomb at Pian Gagliardo has been excavated which has vestiges of a painted decoration of simple ornamental motifs in a large mortuary chamber with a central column.

Burial mound.   Half-cube tombs.

NORCHIA

The Etruscan center was located in the middle section of a road that linked Blera with Tuscania, along a route subsequently followed by the consular road, Via Clodia. Today almost 800 feet of this ancient road is visible north of the ancient settlement, where it passes through a narrow passage known as *Cava Buia* (dark pit), enclosed by sheer walls that reach a height of over 30 feet. Limited vestiges of the ancient town survive, consisting largely of underground passages beneath the area occupied by the thirteenth century castle and a few stretches of the ring of walls.

The monumental tombs situated on the sides of the valleys of the Biedano, Acqualta and Pile rivers, laid out in large cemeteries around the Etruscan town, are of great architectural interest. The tomb of the Three Heads and the Lattanzi Tomb are particularly fascinating. Unfortunately, they are in a poor state of preservation and partly overgrown with bushes.

A view of the rock necropolis.

Part of a tympanum carved with scenes of warriors, from the Hellenistic era necropolis of Norchia. Museo Archeologico, Florence.

CASTEL D'ASSO

Castel d'Asso has been identified with the Roman Axia, one of the strongholds of the territory of Tarquinii. Very few archeological vestiges survive of the Etruscan town, which was set on a steep-sided plateau carved out by the Freddano and Risecco rivers. Like other places in this region, Axia enjoyed a period of considerable affluence in the fourth century, linked to its advantageous position on roads leading inland from the coast. The tombs with elaborate architectural façades that line the valley of the Freddano date from this period, and they have been classified into two types: mock cube tombs (fourth-third centuries BC) and tombs with a smaller façade in front of the main one (third-second centuries BC).

TUSCANIA

Ensured a strategic role from time immemorial by its position at a crossroads, Tuscania also owed its prosperity to its location on a hill at the confluence of the Maschiolo and Marta rivers. One important road linked it with Tarquinii, another with Lake Bolsena and from there with inland Etruria and the valley of the Tiber (mid-sixth century BC). The monumental Cube Tomb in the necropolis of Peschiera is especially interesting as it provides an important clue to Etruscan residential architecture. Excavated from a spur of rock, the tomb has a pitched roof, pediments on the short sides with mock beams and a central door. This leads to three rooms, two of them with carved beams on the ceiling. The large necropolises that are laid out around Tuscania provide evidence for a major crisis during the fifth century BC and a notable cultural revival in the following century. The single-chamber tombs of the local aristocratic families appear to have been in use for several generations, with the bodies interred in sarcophagi carved from nenfro, while the grave goods suggest close contacts with Tarquinii and the Faliscan

View of the rock necropolis of Castel d'Asso.

Façade tomb with false door.

Opposite: Oinochoe from Tuscania, late fourth century BC. Museo Archeologico Nazionale, Tuscania.

Following pages: View of the Tuscania area with the complex of San Pietro on the right.

area. Later on (third-second centuries BC) we find large tombs with platforms for many depositions and terracotta sarcophagi.
In the Roman era Tuscania maintained a thriving economy thanks to its strategic position, as is evident from the luxurious buildings decorated with mosaics that were constructed at the foot of the hill of San Pietro, imposing remains in *opus reticulatum*, stretches of paved road and ruins of baths: the so-called *Bagni della Regina* or Queen's Baths.

View of Tuscania with several sarcophagus lids on display in Piazza Basile.

Nenfro sarcophagi made in Tuscania with reclining figures on their lids. Museo Nazionale, Tuscania and Museo Archeologico, Florence.

ACQUAROSSA

The ancient settlement at Acquarossa stood on a tufaceous plateau bounded by very deep valleys. The town that developed on this site between the seventh and sixth centuries BC has provided precious information about the still little-known Etruscan architecture. The dwellings, quadrangular in shape and with two or three rooms, occupied much of the plateau but were interspersed with areas for farming and grazing. Some of them had a vestibule at the front, or a portico set on wooden columns. The foundations were built of blocks of tufa and the walls of unfired brick, or constructed out of lattices, consisting of vertical poles that supported transverse frameworks The complex wooden structure of the roof was made of beams covered with plain tiles and pantiles, it

was fundamental to control the flow of rainwater which was collected and drained through channels. Special contrivances were also adopted to vent the smoke from the hearth, through a circular opening at the center of one of the tiles whose size could be adjusted by rotation of a disk. In addition to public buildings and roads, a large structure identified as the residence of the aristocratic rulers of the town has been excavated in the archeological area. It was sumptuously decorated with slabs depicting two of Heracles' labors, the slaying of the Nemean lion and the capture of the bull on Crete, and banqueting scenes.

Antefix with a woman's face from zone F of Acquarossa, second half of the sixth century BC. Museo Civico, Viterbo.

Decorative slab representing a Dionysian scene, from zone F of Acquarossa, second half of the sixth century BC. Museo Civico, Viterbo.

The Valley of the Fiora and Albegna

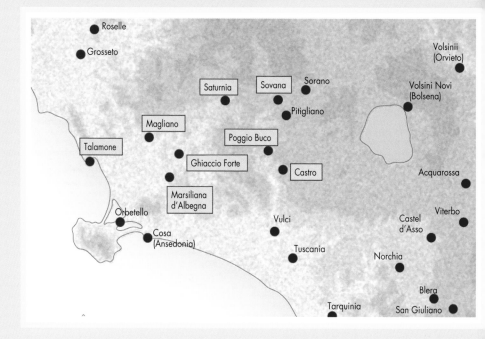

SOVANA

Sovana stands on the site of the ancient city of Suana, a broad tufaceous plateau on the left bank of the Fiora which has been inhabited since the Bronze Age. Its development in the Orientalizing period was due to its strategic location on the important roads linking Vulci with Volsinii and inland Central Etruria. Long stretches of these have survived and are an

impressive sight: called cavoni, they have steep walls cut into the rock that can reach a height of over 80 feet.

Remains of the ancient city (sixth century BC) have been uncovered in the area now occupied by the cathedral, while the ring of walls in *opus quadratum* seems to date from the following century. During the Hellenistic period Suana enjoyed great prosperity, ascribable to intense agricultural exploitation of the territory. The niche-like tomb of the Typhoon (fourth century BC) is located at the end of Via del Cavone, which has Etruscan inscriptions on its walls. Among the graves excavated in the tuff, the Pola Tomb (mid-third century BC) is worthy of note. It too was adorned with a majestic colonnaded portico, although unfortunately only part of this has survived. Another burial place of particular interest is located at Sopraripa, near the sunken road of Via di San Sebastiano. It is a niche called the tomb of the Siren (second half of the third century BC), the pediment of which is decorated with a sculpture of Scylla, the mythological creature that was half woman and half fish. The figure of the deceased reclines in the niche below.

View of the medieval city of Sovana.

The front of the tomb of the Siren in the necropolis of Sopraripa, second half of the third century BC.

Opposite: a view of the sunken road of San Sebastiano at Sovana.

View of some tombs from the seventh-sixth centuries BC. Poggio Buco.

Terracotta basin with figures and horsemen from Valle Rodeta near Pitigliano, second half of the seventh century BC. Museo Archeologico, Florence.

A chamber tomb in the necropolis of the Puntone.

Following pages: Porta Romana with a view of the Via Clodia. Saturnia.

POGGIO BUCO

An important Etruscan settlement stood in a strategic position on the right bank of the Fiora, and controlled the road linking the territory of Vulci with Volsinii and Clusium. Clay architectural slabs adorned with figures have emerged from the sacred area of the ancient center, located on the hill of Le Sparne. A number of dwellings and a paved road have also been brought to light, dating from the late period (second-first centuries BC). The necropolises of Poggio Buco are laid out in a ring around the Etruscan city and contain pit tombs.

CASTRO

Another important Etruscan city stood only about 12½ miles from Vulci, occupying the high ground between the Olpeta and Monache rivers, tributaries of the Fiora. Almost nothing remains of the town: the tomb of the Biga, which contained a rare two-wheeled chariot decorated with bronze plate that is now in the Museo di Villa Giulia; and the tomb of the Bronzes, which had a lavish ornamentation with sculptures of lions, sphinxes and rams produced in Vulci during the first half of the sixth century BC.

SATURNIA

The city owed much of its growth to the advantages of its position at the confluence of the Stellata and Albegna, and its control of the important road that ran along the valley of the same name and linked the territory of Vulci with that of Volsinii, as well as the Amiata area and Clusium. Well tombs have been found at the locality of Sede di Carlo, while the necropolises at Pian di Palma and Puntone have yielded pit, chamber and partition tombs that were in use between the second quarter of the seventh century BC and the middle of the fifth. The conquest of Vulci by the Romans in 280 BC must have wreaked a great deal of destruction on the settlement of Urina as well as Ghiaccio Forte.

GHIACCIO FORTE

The settlement at Ghiaccio Forte was located on an height north of the Albegna River. It emerged during the fourth century BC on a site previously inhabited during the Archaic period and was surrounded by a ring of walls built of crushed stone and unfired brick that must have reached a height of about 20 feet and was about 3000 feet long. Three monumental gates, built of blocks of travertine and nenfro and large rough stones, with vestibules, gave access to the settlement. A sacred area must have been located on the western side of the hill, and already been in use in the late Archaic period, judging by a deposit of anatomical votive offerings in terracotta, bronze statuettes of people making offerings, and animals. The settlement also comprised a very large dwelling that has been identified as the residence of the Statie family: numerous pieces of shot stamped with their mark have been found in various places in the valleys of the Albegna and Fiora.

MAGLIANO

Numerous graves have been found in the hilly territory bounded by the courses of the Albegna and Osa rivers. They were connected with isolated huts, like the one unearthed at Poggio alle Sorche, or with small farming villages, evidently under the control of Vulci.
The two partition tombs with wall paintings discovered at the localities of Le Ficaie (now lost) and, much more recently, Cancellone, are to be attributed to members of the landowning aristocracy. A disk of lead (fifth-fourth centuries BC) with inscriptions engraved in a spiral on both sides that appear to be formulas of dedication to gods of the underworld and the heavens seems to be related to a later burial ground at Santa Maria in Borraccia.

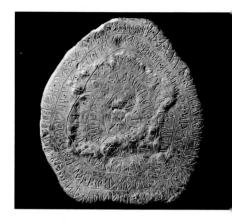

MARSILIANA D'ALBEGNA

Scanty clues as to the location of the ancient settlement have come to light at Uliveto di Bandinella, while the necropolises have yielde materials of great importance. The best know cemetery is the one at Banditella, where abou one hundred tombs have been excavated. Mostly of the pit type and all with an east-we orientation, some are surrounded by circles of stones . The contents of the Circle of the Ivories (675-650 BC) was particularly rich, comprising among other things, a writing set which included the famous ivory tablet with the alphabet engraved along the upper edge, two styli and two scrapers, There were also some particularly sumptuous burials in the necropolis of the Perazzetta, where carts have been found in the tombs.

Lead disk with inscription from Santa Maria in Borraccia near Magliano, fifth-fourth centuries BC. Museo Archeologico, Florence.

Ivory tablet with alphabe engraved on the edge fr the Circle of the Ivories, Marsiliana, 675-650 BC Museo Archeologico, Florence.

TALAMONE

The hill of Talamonaccio, rising high above
the sea and dominating the mouth of the
Osa River and the roadstead of Bengodi,
on whose shores the port must have been
located, played a significant role in the
control of sea routes in the Tyrrhenian.
Excavations of the locality, inhabited as
early as the Copper Age, have yielded
materials from the Late Bronze Age and
the Iron Age, but it does not seem to have
been permanently occupied until the fourth
century BC.
Talamonaccio had a double circle of walls
that were destroyed in the nineteenth
century. At the same time damage was
inflicted on the well-known sanctuary built
at the end of the fourth century BC, of which
parts of the foundations and the podium are
visible today. The most famous monument
excavated in this area is undoubtedly the
terracotta pediment from the second century
BC (on display at Orbetello) that adorned
the sanctuary on the hill of Talamonaccio.

View of the remains of the
temple at Talamonaccio.

Details of the pediment at
Talamonaccio, Adrastus on
his chariot, 150-130 BC.
Museo Civico, Orbetello.

The Tuscan Coast and the *Agro Volterrano*

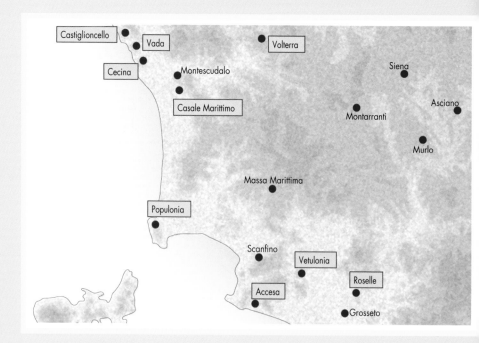

OPULONIA

Populonia, which overlooks the splendid bay of Baratti was founded either by peoples from Corsica or Volterra. Its old name of Pupluna or Fufluna reveals a close connection with Fufluns. Several of the burial grounds (Poggio del Telegrafo, San Cerbone, Casone) that extend over the hills and plateaus facing into the gulf of Baratti date from the oldest phase (ninth century BC). A number of finds of pottery and bronze artifacts from this period indicate contacts with Sardinia, which must have favored an early development of metallurgy.

In the Orientalizing period the necropolises of Populonia were characterized by large burial mounds, each with a circular drum of stone surrounded by paving and a very low dromos providing access to a quadrangular chamber covered with a mock dome. Inhumation appears to have been the only rite used, with the bodies laid out on stone beds adorned with sculpted legs, as can be seen in the tombs of

Tomb of the Cylindrical Boxes in the necropolis of San Cerbone.

Tomb of the Chariots in the necropolis of San Cerbone.

Following pages:
Poggio della Porcareccia, Tomb of the Flabelli. Parco Archeologico, Populonia.

the Carts and the Funeral Beds in particular. The former is the largest tumulus in the necropolis of San Cerbone. The tumulus of the Funeral Beds is located in the necropolis of the Casone. From the late sixth century BC onward aedicule tombs were built in the necropolis of the Casone. The best-preserved example contained a bronze statue of a man making an offering. The tomb is surrounded by other burials inside stone chests that are an indication of the existence of clans based on ties of kinship. Populonia had close ties with the island of Elba, where the iron ore underwent a first stage of smelting before being shipped to the city on the coast. In fact a huge iron-industry district already existed a short distance from the port of Baratti in the sixth century BC, where the Etruscan artisans

engaged in the production of iron worked and lived, while the residences of the wealthy aristocracy were concentrated on the top of the hill. A sure sign of Populonia's affluence is provided by the minting (middle of the fifth century BC) of several series of decorated silver coins. On several levels, in sandstone pit that were no longer quarried, two tombs were found with painted decorations: the Tombs of the *Corridietro* (running wave motif) and the Dolphins, named after the ornamentation of their walls.

Small bronze representing Ajax committing suicide, from the tumulus of the Funeral Beds in the Casone Necropolis, 480-460 BC. Museo Archeologico, Florence.

Above: Aedicula tomb of the Small Bronze of a Ma Making an Offering in the Casone Necropolis.

Below: necropolis of the Grotto.

VETULONIA

Entrance passage of the Pietrera Tumulus, 630-600 BC.

Stone statue of a woman from the Pietrera Tumulus, 630-600 BC. Museo Archeologico, Florence.

Vetulonia (Vetluna or Vatluna in Etruscan) is well documented for the Iron Age (ninth-eighth centuries BC), based on the materials found in the necropolis of Poggio alla Guardia. The well tombs, which only rarely contained more than one burial, have yielded biconical ossuaries and a large number of hut urns. The refinement of the techniques used for the extraction and working of metals in the Orientalizing period was accompanied by marked growth of the population and the economy of Vetulonia, amply documented by extraordinary finds in the necropolises. This was the time when circle tombs appeared. Consisting of one or more pits inside a circle of stones, they contained sumptuous grave goods, including objects imported from Syria, Cyprus and Egypt, along with artifacts from Sardinia like bronze incense boats. From Southern Etruria, on the other hand, came fine objects made of silver. This economic and cultural fervor gave rise to a refined local craft industry, specialized in the working of bronze (vases and tripods with handles shaped like lotus flowers, incense burners, stands for pots) and gold. The techniques of granulation, dusting and embossing were used to transform gold into precious jewelry and ornaments, now on display at the Museo Archeologico in Florence.

In the second half of the seventh century the princely class of Vetulonia built monumental tholos tombs, covered by mounds of earth with conical pillars on top, long access dromoi and central pillars supporting corbel vaults. The Pietrera Tomb (630-600 BC) is an example of this type, located inside a mound with a diameter of almost 200 feet and height of over 45. A broad dromos with two small cells at the sides led to a chamber that must have collapsed shortly after its construction and then had another tomb built on top of it. Another large tomb was the contemporary Little Devil II. Recently restored, new excavations have brought to light parts of stone funeral beds similar to those of the Pietrera, along with numerous objects. The nearby tomb of the Gold Fibula has similar structural characteristics, but is on a more modest scale. The monumental tumulus of Poggio Pelliccia is on the way to Massa Marittima. This is a tholos tomb with a quadrangular chamber at the center and two pit burials on its slopes. Although it was looted in antiquity, the contents of the tomb, now in

the Museo Civico of Vetulonia, include fine Corinthian and Greek-Oriental pottery, which indicates that the tomb was in use between the middle of the seventh and the middle of the fifth centuries BC. The oldest remains of Etruscan Vetluna have been identified in some stretches of the walls in *opus siliceum* (*Mura dell'Arce*) dating from the late sixth to fifth centuries BC, visible almost in the center of the modern town and in the locality of Piantoni. A residential district dating from the third to first centuries BC and known as *Scavi di Città* (excavations in town) has been brought to light at Poggiarello Renzetti. Destroyed in all likelihood by a fire, it is crossed by a paved street, the decumanus, lined by storehouses and atrium dwellings. In one of these, which has been completely excavated, there was a lavish decoration of clay reliefs representing scenes from the myth of Medea. Other urbanized areas have been excavated at the localities of Apparita and Costa dei Lippi, and here too a stretch of paved road and parts of buildings decorated with architectural terracottas have been uncovered.

Excavations of the Hellenistic residential district known as *Scavi di Città*.

Chamber tomb of Poggio Pelliccia in the necropolis of Giuncarico.

Little boat with deer head and various animals along the rim, half of the seventh century BC. Museo Archeologico, Florence.

ACCESA

In the vicinity of the small lake of Accesa, about 4½ miles from Massa Marittima, the remains of an Etruscan town dating from between the late seventh and the sixth centuries BC have been identified. Although still partly under excavation, an area has been equipped with facilities for visitors.
The dwellings brought to light so far are arranged in groups characterized by the presence of a large building surrounded by smaller ones, something that may well reflect the emergence of a social system which already tended to emphasize the role of a dominant class. All that remains of the various structures are the foundations of rough-hewn stones, quarried locally, while no trace has survived of the upper part, Small groups of burials, with pit, chest and chamber tombs, are located a short distance away. The discovery of well tombs indicates that the zone was already occupied in the eighth century, even through there is no direct evidence for settled areas in this period.

ROSELLE

The city spread over two hills facing the former basin of the *Prilewhere Rusellae*, as the Romans called it, had a port. By the middle of the seventh century the city already had a ring of walls built of unfired brick; remains of residential structures with earthen floors and constructed from sun-dried clay can be

Olla and cooking stove, sixth century BC. from the house of the *Impluvium*. Museo Archeologico e d'Arte della Maremma, Grosseto.

Accesa, view of one of the residential districts of the sixth century BC.

dated to the same period. The oldest of these constructions are the "house of the enclosure" and the "house with two rooms," which may have had an important public function for the community as they were not altered in any way even during the Roman era. During the sixth century the city was given a new and massive ring of walls, which is preserved almost in its entirety, almost two miles long and enclosing two hills. Reaching a height of 16½ feet in some places, the walls were built with the *opus siliceum* technique, using very large

blocks cut from the northern side of the hill of Roselle, as the remains of the terracing of the ancient quarries testify. Several gates have been identified in the walls at points corresponding to the roads that connected the city with the north, with the area of Monte Amiata and with the south of Etruria. Several necropolises with burial mounds and chamber tombs, roofed with corbel vaults, were located along these

View of the Roman forum looking toward the southern hill, Roselle.

A view of the buildings from the Roman period near the cardo maximus, Roselle.

outes. A number of tombs have also been excavated in the necropolis of Case di Mota. The large *impluvium* house, covering an area of about 3200 square feet, can be dated to the same period as the construction of the walls. It was laid out around a covered courtyard communicating with eight rooms, including one paved with clay panels that housed a basin to collect rainwater. The remains of the Etruscan period were partly covered up by the boom in building during the Roman era, when the massive structures still visible today were erected, but targeted excavations beneath them have made it possible to bring the oldest vestiges to light. The elliptical amphitheater occupies the top of the northern hill, part of it standing on the ruins of a house from the Hellenistic period (third-second centuries BC). The site overlooks the whole area of the forum, the heart of Roman *Rusellae* where much of city life was conducted. A paved street identified as the cardo maximus, with clear traces of ruts caused by the passage of carts,

runs along the eastern side of the forum. It was interrupted at the point where the basilica stood and transformed into the decumanus, an unusual feature that may have been dictated by the topography of the valley.

VOLTERRA

At the beginning of the Iron Age the most densely populated area was Volterra, where cemeteries with well tombs from as early as the ninth century BC have been found in the area of Le Ripaie, on the southern side of the city. But the elevation on which Volterra stands was the site of other settlements in the Villanovan period, owing to the presence of natural terracing and a view that allowed the inhabitants to observe the valleys of the Cecina, Elsa and Era rivers, while from Guerruccia, near the Balze, it was possible to see the lower valley of the Arno as far as Pisa, and the Apennines and Apuan Alps beyond. In fact various minor Villanovan communities

Well curb, sixth century BC. from the house of the *Impluvium*. Museo Archeologico e d'Arte della Maremma, Grosseto.

Reconstruction of Tomb Q1 of the Ripaie Necropolis at Volterra, second half of the seventh century BC. Museo Etrusco Guarnacci, Volterra.

Etruscan walls. Volterra, Santa Chiara.

Following pages: View of the amphitheater, first century AD, Vallebuona.

emerged on the plateau in the eighth century BC: graves with interesting contents have been found between Guerruccia, Badia and Santa Chiara, on Monte Bradoni and at Poggio alle Croci. The materials from these tombs are on display in the local Museo Guarnacci. From this moment on, numerous minor settlements sprang up in a radial pattern around the city over the course of the following decades, as a consequence of the flight of aristocratic families from the "mother city" into the outlying areas, previously only sparsely inhabited.

Porta all'Arco, third-second centuries BC, Volterra.

Detail of the lid of a cinerary urn known as Urn of the Married Couple, early first century BC. Museo Etrusco "Guarnacci", Volterra.

THE MUSEO ETRUSCO "GUARNACCI" IN VOLTERRA

The typical figure of a local man of learning, Guarnacci founded the museum in 1761. On the ground floor the opening section is devoted to the prehistoric and protohistoric periods (room I), with characteristic materials excavated in the Villanovan necropolises of the early Iron Age, as the pail or *kyathos* in *bucchero* from Monteriggioni, the jewelry from Gesseri di Berignone, the Avile Tite stone *stelae* and the *Lorenzini head*. On the first floor there are many cinerary urns, around 600 in all, grouped by figurative themes. Room XV catches our attention with the *Shadow of the Evening*, as Gabriele D'Annunzio dubbed the slender figure of a youth: the name was later applied to other votive bronzes of similar form. Among the other celebrated pieces in the museum are the lid of a terracotta cinerary urn called the "Urn of the Married Couple" and the famous statue of a woman with a newborn child, known as the "Maffei *kourotrophos*", dating from the third century BC.

VADA

The ancient center of Vada, located on the coast just to the north of the mouth of the Cecina river, already existed in the ninth century BC. A hut village of the Early Iron Age has been discovered in the area of Vada Volaterrana (now the locality of San Gaetano), which was Volterra's port in the Roman era. It acquired an importance that it would retain until the turn of the sixth century AD, that is confirmed by the remains of the Large and Small baths, horrea (warehouses), what was probably a macellum, a schola (seat of an association), a monumental fountain,

Their contents are on display in the archeological museum of Cecina. Tomb A of the cemetery, consisting of a simple square chest of stone slabs, contained a dolium covered with a shield made of bronze plate. The bronze cinerary urn, on the other hand, was covered by a silver bowl and held the bones of the deceased wrapped up with his personal ornaments in a linen cloth (a custom mentioned in Homeric poetry). There is not any clear evidence of well-organized urban structures, such as the residential areas of Piano di Castello, until the sixth century BC. It was here that the oldest buildings stood, protected by the first, short ring of walls of the same period around the acropolis, less than one mile long. In the first half of the fifth century a second ring of walls was erected, this time about 1¼ miles long. There were both dwellings as well as places of worship on the acropolis. Bucchero ware and Attic red-figure pottery have often been found in the structures of the former. The production of cinerary urns was also important, which were made from limestone and tuff in the fourth and third centuries BC. The older type (second half of the fourth century BC) were chests with lids in the form of a pitched roof, where reclining figures were represented idealized images of the deceased. In the Hellenistic era the acropolis of Volterra was restructured, with the construction of two adjacent temples. All that remains of the older one to the north, dating from the third century BC, is the base, but this is sufficient to make out its plan with a *cella* and *alae* preceded by two rows of four columns. The other place of worship, built in the second century BC, was set on a tall podium with a flight of steps and had the appearance of a Greek temple.

and buildings which can now be visited in the Archeological Area of San Gaetano di Vada. The materials from the port district are on display in the civic archeological museum of Rosignano Marittimo, along with prehistoric and protohistoric finds, the contents of Etruscan-Hellenistic tombs at Castiglioncello, the tombs at Pian dei Lupi and objects that have been recovered from the seabed.

THE TERRITORY OF VOLTERRA AND CASALE MARITTIMO

The vast inland territory of Volterra, already inhabited in the Early Iron Age, also underwent changes between the eighth and seventh centuries BC. Tumuli, such as that of Montecalvario at Castellina in Chianti, and necropolises, such as the Casone di Monteriggioni, have been found at the settlements that dominated communications with inland Etruria and the passes through the Apennines. In the area of the western Volterran region, groups of tombs bear witness to the existence of settlements from the end of the eighth century onward, at Pomarance, Cerreta, Totolla and Guardistallo. The famous impasto cinerary urn, dated from the first half of the seventh century BC now in the archeological museum of Cecina, came from Montescudaio. But the most exceptional archeological discoveries have been made at Casale Marittimo where the necropolis of Casa Nocera has been identified.

Kyathos of Monteriggioni with inscription, mid-seventh century BC. Museo Etrusco "Guarnacci", Volterra.

Small bronze known as *Shadow of the Evening*, third century BC. Museo Etrusco "Guarnacci", Volterra.

Following pages: Funerary sculptures from the necropolis at Casale Marittimo, mid-seventh century BC. Museo Archeologico, Cecina and Cinerary urn of Montescudaio with banqueting scene, mid-seventh century BC. Museo Archeologico, Cecina.

CECINA, CASTIGLIONCELLO AND SURROUNDINGS

The Roman villa in the archeological park of San Vincenzino, near Cecina, is traditionally attributed to the Caecina family. When it was built, about 30 BC, it had the plan of a typical urban villa. The baths and summer triclinium were added later (second-third centuries AD). Evidence of life at the site, which remained inhabited up until the fifth century AD, is provided by the cemetery and small antiquarium which dates from the first half of the third century BC. Table pottery and precious objects in gold and silver have been found in these tombs.

Casole, in the upper valley of the Elsa river, was an important settlement at the center of a series of minor sites, where scattered tombs have been discovered along a route that linked them to the road from Monteriggioni to Volterra. To the south of Volterra, at Sasso Pisano, an Etruscan complex of temples and baths has been excavated and can now be visited. Built in the third century BC, it was restored after a landslide and then remained in use up until the third century AD. The public importance of the place has suggested identification of the buildings with the *Aquae Volaterranae* marked on the *Peutinger Table*, a medieval copy of a map of the Roman empire. The public complex of Torretta Vecchia near Collesalvetti was continuously inhabited between the first century BC and the middle of the sixth century AD, with clearly identifiable remains of the Augustan era, including those of small heated baths. Abandoned in the middle of the sixth century, during the Gothic War, it can now be visited by prior arrangement.

Interior of the southern tomb, Montecalvario Tumulus at Castellina in Chianti, seventh century BC.

Bronze shield from Tomb A at Casale Marittimo, eighth-seventh centuries BC. Museo Archeologico, Cecina.

The Sienese Valdichiana, the Valley of the Ombrone and Eastern Etruria

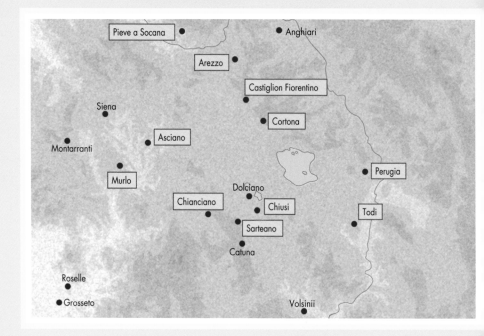

CHIUSI

In ancient times it was known as the city of Camars. The hill to the west of the Chiana River, where the Etruscans would build their city, appears to have been inhabited during the Bronze Age, probably because of its strategic position. In the subsequent Iron Age (ninth century BC), a number of small settlements grew up in the territory of Chiusi, while the later Orientalizing necropolises brought to light on the hillsides around the town mark the increase in population. They contain interments in jars, usually with individual depositions. At this time the city's aristocratic families buried their dead

with lavish grave goods in monumental chamber tombs excavated in sandstone or built from blocks of stone, usually covered by mounds. The oldest remains connected with the city have been identified at Petriolo, a no longer urbanized area where recent excavations have identified a sort of artisans' district filled with potteries. In fact the economic and cultural fervor that characterized Camars over the course of the sixth century favored a lively local handicraft industry that

Interior of the Tomb of the Female Pilgrim from Chiusi, late fourth-early third centuries BC.

Urna Larth Sentinates, Caesa of the Tomb of the Female Pilgrim from Chiusi, early third century BC. Museo Archeologico Nazionale, Chiusi.

specialized chiefly in the production of richly
decorated bucchero ware and objects in ivory.
At the same time it encouraged the importation
of luxury objects from Greece (such as the
extraordinary François Vase) or Southern Etruria.
Toward the end of the sixth century BC the city
attained the peak of its power and a high level
of prosperity based on the cultivation of cereals,
vines and olives in the fertile countryside. This
affluence is also reflected in a number of tombs
with wall paintings dating from the first half of
the fifth century, of which only the ones in the
tombs of the Monkey (480 BC) and the Hill (470
BC) have been preserved. The city's aristocrats
remained wealthy into the third century BC, as
is apparent from the Tomb of the Female Pilgrim
(open to the public) where several generations of
the Sentinate family were buried. The alabaster
urns and the sarcophagi that can still be seen
inside the tomb, just as its discoverers found
them, are examples of the typical local production
of the early decades of the second century

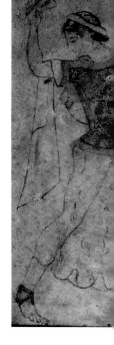

Two images of the
frescoes of the Tomb of the
Hill, 470 BC.

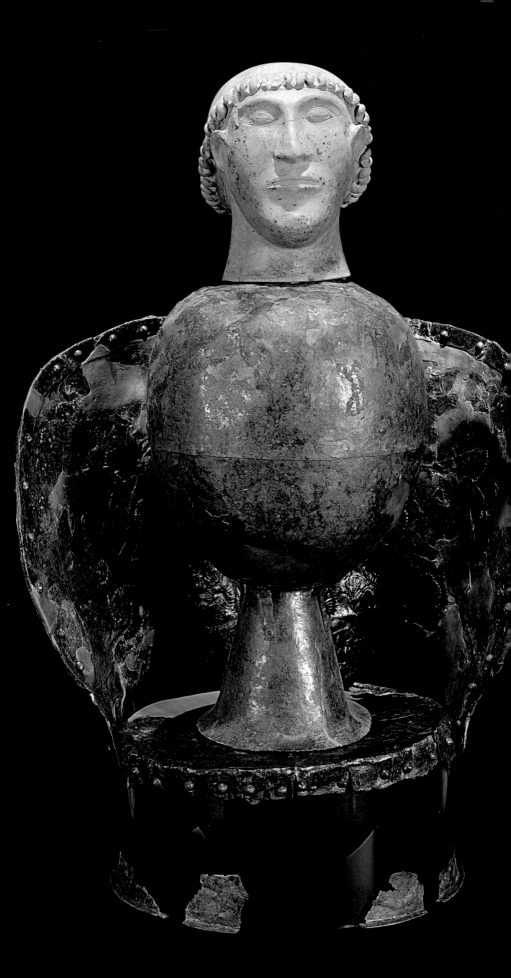

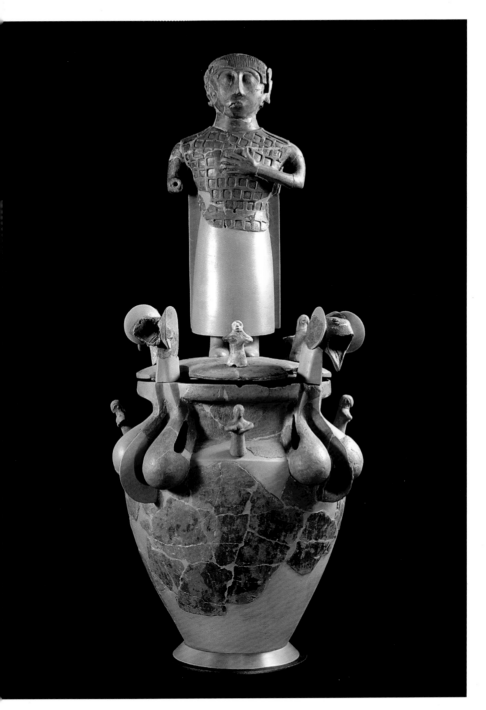

THE MUSEO ARCHEOLOGICO NAZIONALE IN CHIUSI

The museum in Chiusi was opened in 1871, displaying materials donated by the local aristocracy and clergy. One of the most interesting Canopic jars on show is the one known as Dolciano (after the name of the place it was found): dating from the closing decades of the 7th century, it has a bronze throne and ossuary and a clay head. The *Paolozzi Ossuary* with a female figure on the lid can be assigned to the same period. The display continues with figured pottery of Attic and Etruscan manufacture, including a red-figure *skyphos* with scenes from the *Odyssey:* Telemachus and Penelope at the loom and the recognition of Ulysses by his nurse Eurycleia.

Opposite: Canopic jar of Dolciano, last decades of the seventh century BC. Museo Archeologico Nazionale, Chiusi.

Paolozzi Ossuary from Dolciano, near Chiusi, 620 BC. Museo Archeologico Nazionale, Chiusi.

CHIANCIANO

The oldest vestiges uncovered in the area of Chianciano provide evidence of remarkable well-being during the Orientalizing period, as is apparent from the large necropolis of Tolle, still under excavation, where several hundred seventh century tombs have been found so far. Particularly common are Canopic vases (ossuaries with anthropomorphic features characteristic of the Chiusi area) deposited in jars, box and chamber tombs, along with large amounts of locally made and imported pottery. Already famous in antiquity for its numerous mineral springs, Chianciano was the seat, during the Etruscan era, of important sanctuaries linked to the cult of water. In addition to the remains of a place of worship dedicated first to Apollo and then to Diana, extraordinary fragments of a bronze offering to the gods with statues of men (fifth century BC) and women on a chariot (fourth century BC) have been found in the locality of Sillene. At another sanctuary located at I Fucoli, part of a terracotta pediment (second century BC) has been discovered with exquisitely molded statues that are now on display at the local Museo Civico Archeologico. Particularly rich tombs, now partly open to the public, were discovered in the Pedata Necropolis, where the famous cinerary statues of fetid limestone

representing, respectively, a woman holding a child (the so-called *Mater Matuta*) and a dead man accompanied by the winged god Vanth, displaying the scroll of destiny, were found.

SARTEANO

The site of important vestiges from prehistoric times, Sarteano is also known for its vast necropolises reflecting the great prosperity of the Orientalizing period. These burial grounds extend along the hillsides of Solaia, Poggio Rotondo and Macchiapiana. The considerable affluence of the local aristocracy is apparent from the discovery of numerous Canopic vases in jar and chamber tombs, some of them housing double interments, with substantial grave goods. Finds of considerable value from later centuries have also been made and for the most part can be seen at the local Museo Civico Archeologico. They reflect a high degree of prosperity: an exceptional example of this is the recent discovery at the locality of Pianacce of a second painted tomb from the final decades of the fourth century BC,

Lid of cinerary urn representing the deceased and Vanth, second half of the fifth century BC. Museo Archeologico, Florence.

Opposite: *Mater Matuta*, from the Pedata Necropolis at Chianciano, circa 470 BC. Museo Archeologico, Florence.

called the tomb of the Infernal Quadriga. The graves of the Hellenistic period continue to bear witness to the vitality of the region of Sarteano, with their sarcophagi made of alabaster and travertine and numerous urns of high quality, while the funerary architecture is extremely varied, with dromoi sometimes of great length used to house a large number of burials in small niches in the walls. An interesting example of this can be seen at the burial complex excavated at Mulin Canale. During the Roman era

Reconstruction of the tomb with Canopic jars in the Macchiapiana Necropolis, Sarteano, late seventh-early sixth centuries BC. Museo Civico Archeologico, Sarteano.

Face of the demon Charun in the tomb of the Infernal Quadriga, last decades of the fourth century BC. Pianacce Necropolis, Sarteano.

Opposite: Two faces of the cippus in fetid limestone from Sant'Angelo, Sarteano, last decades of the sixth century BC. Museo Civico Archeologico, Sarteano.

imposing villas decorated with figurative slabs and mosaics were built. Significant remains of these can be seen at the locality of Peschiera.

MURLO

In Etruscan times the hill of Poggio Civitate, bounded on the west by the course of the Creole, a tributary of the Ombrone river, was the site of an important aristocratic residence. Dating to the seventh century BC, the large building with a quadrangular plan was reconstructed during the sixth century. It had a large open courtyard at the center surrounded by a wooden colonnade, off which numerous rooms used for household activities opened. The architectural decoration (reassembled in the local museum) set on top of the roof consisted of seated male figures wearing large hats, alternated with sphinxes. The base of the walls was built of stone and the upper part of unfired clay, supported by an internal framework of branches and reeds.

Another large building was discovered at the southern end of the plateau and has been identified as a workshop used for the production of pottery, decorative slabs and small objects in bronze, ivory, horn and bone. Other parts of the same building must have been used for processing foodstuffs.

Acroterion from Poggio Civitate, Murlo.

Reconstruction of a section of the roof of the princely palace at Murlo, early decades of the sixth century BC. Antiquarium di Poggio Civitate, Murlo.

SCIANO

The Etruscan settlement in the area of sciano, the exact location of which is nknown, went through a period of great rosperity between the seventh and sixth enturies BC, as the finds made at the umulus of the Mulinello have recently evealed. The importance of this center erived from the presence of an aristocratic lass whose wealth came from farming and rom exploitation of the travertine quarries, vhich appear to have been worked since as ar back as the end of the seventh century 3C. The fortunate position in the valley f the Ombrone, which permitted easy ommunications with Vetulonia and Rusellae, nust have favored the development of the ettlement in the vicinity of Asciano. The mported painted vases of Greek and Etruscan nanufacture found in the tombs excavated t Poggio Pinci, dating from between the fth and the first centuries BC, testify to the ontinuing vitality of this area. The existence f important families connected with the anded aristocracy is documented by tombs ke the large one of the Hepni, in which round thirty people were buried, the last of hem in the Augustan age.

CORTONA

The ancient settlement occupied the same site as the medieval and Renaissance city, on a spur of Monte Sant'Egidio overlooking the fertile Valdichiana and about 6 miles from the northern shore of Lake Trasimeno. The city's prosperity during the Orientalizing period (seventh century BC) is amply documented by the large burial mounds (known locally as *meloni* or *melons*) visible at the foot of the hill on which it stands. The large one called the *Melone II del Sodo* is spectacular: here two chamber tombs were discovered at different times, unfortunately both of them looted. The first has a long dromos with two vestibules in sequence leading to seven cells, six at the sides and one at the end. The other, a quadrangular tomb, from a later date, housed inhumations in stone sarcophagi and cinerary urns. The importance of this mound stems essentially from the presence of a large altar-terrace: one of a kind, it has a flight of steps leading to a platform originally covered by a roof of wood and brick decorated with figured slabs. The extraordinary parapet has double volutes with sculptural elements at the base representing a warrior locked in combat with a wild beast. The other tombs discovered at a short distance from the city are from a later date (second century BC) and consist of mortuary

ltar platform of the umulo del Sodo, 80-560 BC, Asciano.

Following pages: Facing slab with scene of assembly, early decades of the sixth century BC.

Antiquarium di Poggio Civitate, Murlo.

chambers built out of blocks of stone and covered with tunnel vaults, known locally as the *Tanella di Pitagora* and *Tanella Angori;* all that remains of the latter is the base. Substantial sections of the ancient city's walls, constructed out of large blocks of millstone grit, have survived, along with a few remains of buildings. The celebrated bronze chandelier (fourth century BC) comes from what may have been a sanctuary at the nearby locality of Fratta. It has a complex ornamentation with figures of harpies alternated with satyrs and a large, beautifully crafted Gorgon's head at the center.

CASTIGLION FIORENTINO

Substantial remains of an Etruscan settlement of the Archaic period that had probably had the function of controlling Clanis valley below have recently been identified inside the majestic keep of

A detail of the bronze chandelier from Fratta, Cortona, fourth century BC. Museo dell'Accademia Etrusca, Cortona.

Tanella di Pitagora tomb, second century BC.

Castiglion Fiorentino, between Cortona and Arezzo. The archeological data shows a sanctuary, adorned with slabs painted with Gorgon's heads, dating from the late fifth-early fourth centuries BC. The place of worship was still in use in the second century BC, the date of the potsherds and several slabs with floral motifs in relief that have been found there.
In the Hellenistic period the small town was surrounded with massive defensive walls.

AREZZO

Located at the conjunction of the Valdichiana foothills with the Casentino mountains, the city owes its origin to its favorable geographic position, at an obligatory point of passage along the routes to Emilia Romagna and the Po Valley in the north and the Tiber valley to the east. Faint traces of a ring of walls of uncertain date show that the ancient city stood in the area now comprised between the Medici Fortress and the cathedral. Its economy must have been based on agricultural exploitation of the plain below, and the settlement was probably founded in the second half of the sixth century BC, as confirmed by the votive offerings found at Poggio al Sole, the deposit of votive offerings at Fonte Veneziana, seat of a sanctuary in the fifth century, which contained bronze statuettes of kouroi and korai, and a large collection of ex-votos discovered near the bastion of Porta San Lorentino. The celebrated sculpture of the

Chimera, a masterpiece of fourth century Etruscan bronze work discovered in the mid sixteenth century during the construction of the city walls, also comes from this area. The military pressure exerted on the cities of Etruria by the Romans at the beginning of the third century was brought to bear on Arezzo too, and the city was forced to pay a very heavy tribute to obtain peace. The

Votive head from the deposit on Via della Società Operaia in Arezzo, second-first centuries BC and the *Chimera of Arezzo*, 400-350 BC. Museo Archeologico, Florence.

Following pages: facing slab with warriors from Piazza San Jacopo in Arezzo, early fifth century BC. Museo Nazionale Archeologico, Arezzo.

sanctuary of Castelsecco, visible on the hill of San Cornelio a little less than 2 miles from the city, evidently also dates from a period of renewed construction. It was linked with a theater with its own scene building, decorated with terracotta slabs. The imposing remains of an amphitheater that could hold up to 8000 spectators survive from Roman Arretium, still flourishing in the first century AD.

Small bonzes, seventh-sixth centuries BC. Museo Archeologico Nazionale, Arezzo.

Roman theater of Vallebuona, early first century AD, Arezzo.

PIEVE A SOCANA

Remains of an Etruscan sanctuary have been brought to light at the medieval church of Sant'Antonino at Pieve a Socana, bearing witness to the continuity of worship at this sacred place. A large sacrificial altar and a flight of steps have been identified as belonging to the ancient sanctuary. The building was adorned with terracottas datable to the fifth century BC, and some small altars and large stone disks with dedications to the Sun come from the same period. The presence of a

number of terracotta antefixes indicate that
it was redecorated in the second century BC.
The sanctuary must have served the religious
needs of the rural population and travelers
on the important road along the right bank
of the Arno to Mount Falterona. The loss of
this route's importance brought about a rapid
decline of the sanctuary, which was abandoned
at the beginning of the first century BC.

Parish church
of Sant'Antonino:
in the foreground, remains
of the Etruscan sanctuary
of the fifth century BC.

Large stone disk with
dedication to the sun from
the Etruscan sanctuary of
Pieve a Socana, fifth century
BC. Museo Archeologico
Nazionale, Arezzo.

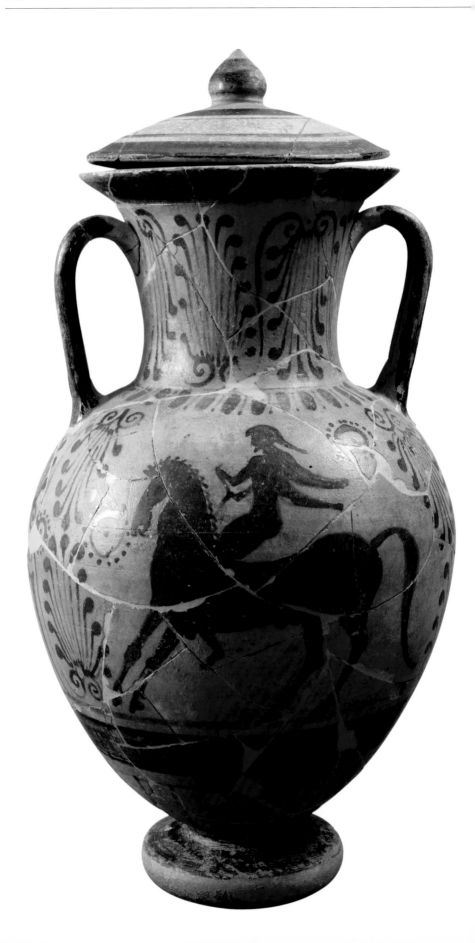

PERUGIA

Its strategic position at the junction of the lines of communication between the upper valley of the Tiber and the Umbrian Valley contributed to the growth of the city. After 90 BC it became a Roman municipium and was assigned to the Tromentina tribe. A half century later, after giving refuge to Mark Anthony's brother Lucius, it was besieged by Octavian (Augustus), taken by storm and burned (40 BC). It was then reconstructed and given the name of Augusta Perusia. Owing to the continuity of life through the medieval and modern eras, part of the ancient city's ring of walls has been preserved: built of blocks of travertine, it was almost 2 miles long and had monumental gates. Two of them have survived, both from the second half of the third century BC: the Gate of Mars, incorporated into the

Rocca Paolina and adorned with busts of Jupiter and the Dioscuri and horse's heads, and the Gate of Augustus, flanked by two Roman-built towers, with a round arch surmounted by a decoration of shields and pilasters. The cemeteries have yielded evidence from as far back as the Iron Age, in particular the huge necropolis of the Palazzone. The necropolis also contains the monumental hypogeum of the Velimna-Volumni family with burials dating from between the second and first centuries BC. The tomb, one of the most interesting of the late Etruscan era, consists of a central vestibule surrounded by four cells and a corridor at the back leading to three more mortuary chambers. It illustrates the interior of a house from the Hellenistic period, with the vestibule covered by a pitched ceiling, the wooden structure of which is realistically rendered, and a pediment at the rear adorned with an emblem in relief between two heads. The central chamber, decorated with a Gorgon's head on the ceiling, housed the oldest burials, in cinerary urns of remarkable refinement. The urn of the family founder, Arnth Velimnes, an important magistrate in second century BC Perugia, is particularly sumptuous, with the figure of the deceased reclining on the lid, supported by two winged demons (lase), standing guard at a painted door.

Gate of Mars, detail, second half of the third century BC.

Opposite: Amphora from Tomb 172, necropolis of Palazzone. Perugia, Museo Archeologico, Perugia.

Interior of the hypogeum of the Volumni, necropolis of Palazzone, second century BC.

TODI

Todi stands on an elevation between the Tiber and the small Naia and Rio rivers, in an ideal position to exercise control over the important watercourse and the road that led to Volsinii. The Etruscan name of this ancient Umbrian city, Tutere (tute = boundary), is a reference to its geographic location along the border. The city entered the Etruscan political sphere in the fifth century, when it experienced a period of great economic prosperity that was to last for two centuries and even prompted it to mint a coin of its own inscribed with the name Tuter. The graves in the necropolis of the Peschiera date from this period. The deposit of votive offerings in the suburban sanctuary of Monte Santo is datable to the fourth century BC, and it was here that the famous bronze statue known as the Mars of Todi, now in the Vatican Museums, was found. Todi's affluence is well documented up until the third century BC, when it came under Roman rule.

Gold earrings from the necropolis of Peschiera, Todi, early third century BC. Museo Nazionale Etrusco di Villa Giulia, Rome.

Opposite: Mars of Todi, early fourth century BC. Museo Gregoriano Etrusco, Vatican.

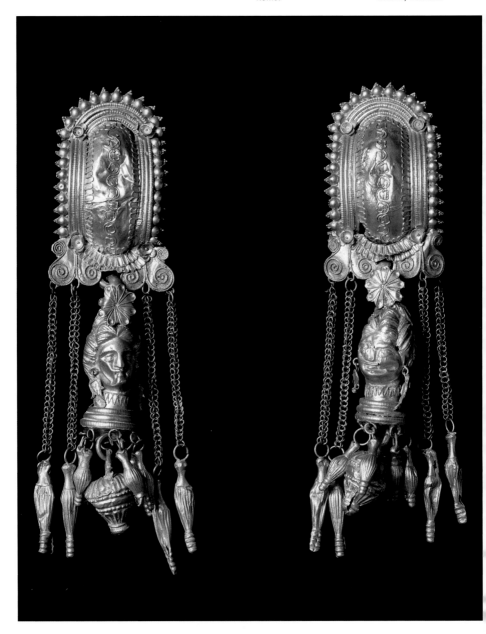

Northern Etruria

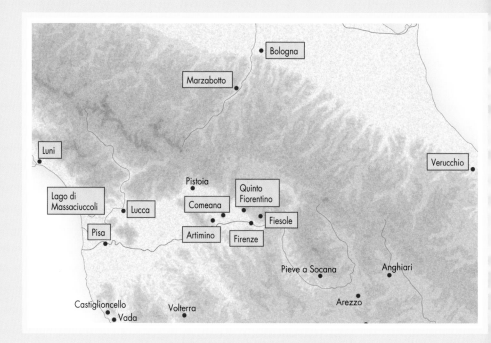

LORENCE

A small group of tombs in the center of
he city undoubtedly belonged to scattered
ettlements, and may have been of a family
haracter in some way. A similar situation has
een identified in the center of Florence, where
ix well tombs with biconical jars and vases
rom the eighth century BC were discovered
n the nineteenth century. More recently, other
inds from destroyed graves have been made,
longside fragments of pottery with geometric
lecoration imported from Greece or southern
taly. The provenance of these last finds is
i clear indication of the role of commercial
unction that the Florentine settlement
epresented from its origins, as a useful
rossroads on the routes between northern
Etruria and the Apennine passes. The Roman
orum was located on the site of what is now
Piazza della Repubblica, baths and dye houses
occupied Piazza Signoria, while the remains of
he theater are located under Palazzo Vecchio,
next to the city walls.

Cinerary urn with bowl-lid
from the tomb 4 of the
Gambrinus Necropolis,
Florence, mid-eighth
century BC. Museo di
Firenze com'era, Florence.

Jar with cinerary urn from
tomb 6 of the Gambrinus
Necropolis, Florence,
mid-eighth century BC.
Museo di Firenze com'era,
Florence.

THE MUSEO ARCHEOLOGICO NAZIONALE IN FLORENCE

On the ground floor, there is an interesting garden laid out in a typically antiquarian style. Underneath the numerous varieties of tree and flowers with which it is planted, in fact, lie genuine Etruscan tombs – such as the one in an Oriental style from Casale Marittimo, dismantled and then reconstructed here – as well as reproductions of graves like the Inghirami Tomb in Volterra. Other features include the Tomb of the Little Devil and the front of a small temple, inspired by the shrine of Ponte Rotto near Vulci, as well as smaller tombs and numerous sculptures. The Etruscan collection commences in room XIV, the so-called Gallery of Bronzes; outstanding among these, in addition to numerous votive statuettes, are the large bronzes brought to light

in the 16th century, formerly the pride of the Medicean collection. The first of them is the *Chimera* from Arezzo dating from the 4th cent BC. Discovered in 1553, its serpent's tail is the fruit of a restoration traditionally attributed to Benvenuto Cellini, although without any hard evidence. The large sculpture must once have been part of a group, of which the part made up of the winged horse ridden by Bellerophon has been lost, while the inscription on the monster's right paw tells us that the work was a votive offering to Jupiter-Tinia. A short distance away stands the statue of an orator known as the *Arringatore* from Sanguineto sul Trasimeno, brought to Tuscany in an adventurous fashion following its discovery

François Vase from Fonte Rotella, Chiusi, 560 BC. Museo Archeologico Nazionale, Florence.

n 1566. On the same story there are rooms
displaying Etruscan stone sculptures, with
small chest-shaped cinerary urns, sarcophagi
(including that of the "Obese Etruscan"),
cinerary statues and the pediment of a rock
tomb from Norchia. Outstanding among these
exhibits is the celebrated "Sarcophagus of the
Amazons" from Tarquinia. Another masterpiece
is the famous *François Vase*, made by the potter
Ergotimos and the vase painter Cleitias, who
decorated it with superimposed friezes of
mythological scenes. Dating from around 570
BC, the pot is painted with black figures and
embellished with incised details.

Inghirami Tomb at
Volterra, second century
BC. reconstructed in
the garden, Museo
Archeologico, Florence.

*Sarcophagus of the Obese
Etruscan*, detail, early
third century BC. Museo
Archeologico Nazionale,
Florence.

Arringatore, 100-80
BC. from Sanguineto
sul Trasimeno. Museo
Archeologico Nazionale,
Florence.

QUINTO FIORENTINO AND THE MUGELLO VALLEY

Two monumental chamber tombs, constructed of stone blocks and surmounted by an enormous mound of earth have survived in Quinto Fiorentino. The better conserved of the two, the Montagnola Tomb, has a diameter of almost 200 feet, and is ringed by a drum of stone slabs with a circumference of over 400 feet. A long open passageway, or dromos, leads to the inner vestibule through a portal formed by two monoliths for jambs and another for the lintel. The walls of the rectangular vestibule, originally plastered and painted brown, blue and red, still have graffiti with stars, animals, plants and letters. The doors to two small cells were placed here at the sides. A ogival doorway at the back of the vestibule leads to the circular cell, the sturdy central pillar still bears inscriptions and nails where some elements of the grave goods were hung. Looted in antiquity, the Tomb of the Montagnola has unfortunately yielded only a few fragmentary remains of its original contents. The tomb of the Mula, now underneath the villa of the same name where it forms the cellar, is only a short distance away. Discovered a very long time ago, in addition to a majestic portal that leads into the round cell with a diameter of 30 feet without

a central pillar, perhaps since ancient times. The situation was very similar in the Mugello, where archeological research has been resumed in recent years with considerable success, as the exhibitions staged at the museums of Bruscoli, Palazzuolo sul Senio and Sant'Agata demonstrate. Without listing the many sporadic finds, it will suffice to mention those of the settlement at Poggio di Colla near Vicchio and San Piero a Sieve.

Corridor inside the Montagnola Tomb, Quinto Fiorentino, late seventh century BC.

Interior of the Mula Tomb, Quinto Fiorentino, late seventh century BC.

Amphora with lid from the Boschetti Tomb, 670-650 BC. Museo Archeologico, Artimino.

Bucchero censer from Tumulus C of the necropolis of Prato di Rosello, last two decades of the seventh-early sixth century BC. Museo Archeologico, Artimino.

ARTIMINO AND COMEANA

More discoveries of great importance have been made at Artimino, where a hill with three small but distinct peaks was the site of a settlement as far back as the seventh century BC. In addition to finds from the inhabited area, located during the Orientalizing period in the area of the Paggeria or Servants' Quarters of the Medici villa, there are remains of tombs in the cemeteries at Prato di Rosello and Comeana. The Boschetti Tomb, now open to the public, consisted of a short passageway that led to a vestibule and an almost cubic space measuring 5½ feet along each axis. The Montefortini Tumulus, on the other hand, has the proportions of an artificial hill. About 200 feet in diameter and almost 50 high, it is supported by a drum of stones that is only partially visible, from which an altar-terrace projected for the exposition of the dead and their grave goods. The mound contains two tombs from different times, one of them open to the public. The oldest, dating from the mid-seventh century, is located at the center of the mound and, like the Montagnola Tomb at Quinto, has a circular cell with a corbelled vault. It has a diameter of 23 feet and a central pillar. The new tomb,

now accessible, was created in the place of the corridor, preceded by an open passageway 42 feet long and a vestibule covered with projecting stones. These lead, through a movable door that has now vanished, to a rectangular cell over 13 feet long, also covered with a corbeled vault and fitted with the same stone "shelf" running around the walls as is the older, circular tholos.

FIESOLE

Numerous remains of both Villanovan and Orientalizing pottery, including distinctive two-horned handles with hollow appendages come from the same area, although lacking their original context. These finds are displayed in the local civic archeological museum. The pottery of the Orientalizing period unearthed at Fiesole should be seen in relation to the remains of buildings that were destroyed by the subsequent creation of a sacred area but which are recognizable as dwellings. They may have been used in the final part of the seventh century. Here, at the beginning of the sixth century BC, we see an exponential increase in the quantity of finds, as well as a radical change in their typology. The refined finishing and the uniformity of these pots, made on the wheel from clay of high quality, clearly shows them to be the products of true workshops of craftsmen, the existence of which indicates the presence of a large population, capable of sustaining substantial and enduring demand. In any case Fiesole was, in the early sixth century BC, a social structure made up of a large number of individuals occupying a very large area, living in quadrangular houses. A small sacred building was erected during the fifth century and renovated during the Hellenistic era on the southern side of Fiesole, near Villa Marchi. Over forty votive

Sandstone stele from Travignoli near Fiesole, early fifth century BC. Museo Archeologico, Fiesole.

Remains of the Etruscan temple, fourth-third centuries BC, Fiesole.

Bronze helmet from the acropolis of Fiesole, first half of the fifth century BC. Museo Etnografico Missionario, Fiesole.

Below: Lion's Head on stone from the acropolis of Fiesole, sixth-fifth centuries BC. Museo Etnografico Missionario, Fiesole.

bronzes were found here, along with pottery and fragments of aes rude (lumps of bronze used as currency before the introduction of coins). Other finds come from the hill of San Francesco (Sant'Apollinare). The walls form an impressive line of defense over 1½ miles long. The longest surviving parts are on the northern and eastern sides, but shorter stretches are also present to the south and on the citadel. The destruction of the northern sacellum of Fiesole by a fire, around the middle of the fifth century BC, may have been followed shortly afterward by the construction of the large Etruscan temple, which can now be visited in the archeological area. The chronology of this building, traditionally dated to the end of the fourth century, is now undergoing revision. During its construction efforts were made not to desecrate the remains of the small shrine, over which the innermost cell of the new temple was situated. It had a larger cell at the center and two narrower rooms at the sides, the alae, while the walls extended as far as the building's façade. Thus its pronaos was closed at the sides, with only two large columns at the front. The complex was set on a tall podium, from which a flight of steps led down to the altar in front. Unlike the majority of Etruscan temples, the one in Fiesole had walls built of stone instead of unfired brick, which has allowed more of it to survive. Protected from the infiltration of water by a complicated system of drains that discharged outside the city, the temple was embellished in successive phases by a pediment with scenes of combat and lateral antefixes with small applied heads (third-second centuries BC), as well as two rooms located symmetrically at the sides. These were used to receive worshipers, who left small bronzes and pottery as votive offerings. The six Etruscan tombs

in the only cemetery to have been identified in the city, on Via del Bargellino, also belong to this historical phase: dating from the end of the fourth century and reutilized up until the period of Romanization, only four of them are still visible. Once again it was a great fire that brought this temple to the end of its existence, perhaps during the destruction of the city in 90 BC, which was followed in 80 by the founding of a Roman colony on the site by Sulla's veterans. The area of the Etruscan temple was buried under several meters of earth, and a new but larger building was created on a similar plan to the previous one, endowed with a grand flight of steps and a colonnaded portico.

GARFAGNANA AND LUNIGIANA

The presence of numerous mountainous areas has favored human settlement in caves and gorges since prehistoric times. Some of the most significant finds have been made at Tecchia di Equi, in the vicinity of Equi Terme in Lunigiana, which has yielded stone artifacts from the Middle Paleolithic age that are attributed to the Mousterian culture (named after the locality of Le Moustier in France) and document the presence of Neanderthals. Later frequented by populations of the Copper Age, this rock shelter connected to a cave is now open to the public, and part of the material found in it is on display in the *Museo del Territorio dell'Alta Valle Aulella* at Casola in Lunigiana. The Garfagnana was also occupied in the Paleolithic age, as the oldest materials in the archeological museum at Castelnuovo Garfagnana demonstrate, although interesting finds from the sandpits around Massaciuccoli Lake prove that it was not just the high ground that offered shelter to human beings at the time. The occupation of these sites was far more extensive in the Copper and Bronze Ages. An example of the former is the grave from the Grotta dell'Inferno at Vecchiano, now reconstructed in the civic museum of Viareggio, while the second case is represented by the *Buca delle Fate*. Among the typical finds of the Chalcolithic era are precious triangular daggers made of copper, metal bracelets and axes, and three types of contemporary pottery. Some unusual sculptures from the early Metal

Ages have been found in a limited area between the valley of the Magra and the Apuan Alps. Known as the stelae-statues of Lunigiana, they have limited parallels with other artifacts of the Alpine area and Europe in general. The oldest examples, dating from the Copper Age (3400-2000 BC), have been divided into the *Pontevecchio* or A type and *Malgrate* or B type. The former has the characteristic appearance of a large slab of stone rounded at the top, with simple features of the human face reproduced in the upper part but no sign of a neck; the latter, in contrast, has a short and distinct neck, underneath a semicircular head. On both types arms and distinguishing attributes, such as weapons, are represented in bas-relief. While the function of these sculptures is not clear, it is possible that they were placed inside sacred precincts, not necessarily used as cemeteries. A third type (called Reusa or C), much closer to a rudimentary statue with exclusively male connotations, is believed to date from the Iron Age, as is suggested by the inscriptions in the Etruscan alphabet carved on some specimens. A wide range of these sculptures can be seen in the *Museo delle Statue Stele Lunigianesi*, housed in the picturesque Castello del Piagnaro at Pontremoli, while there are two more examples in the museum at Casola in Lunigiana.

Several Copper-Age stelae of the Pontevecchio type from Lunigiana, Museo delle Statue Stele Lunigianesi, Pontremoli.

PISA

In this context Pisa appears to have been a center of great importance from the ninth century BC onward, the period of several Villanovan tombs and traces of an inhabited area within the limits of the modern city. In December 1998, while building the operational headquarters of the State Railroads at the station of San Rossore, an exceptional archeological discovery was made. The remains of the urban harbor of the Etruscan and Roman city were brought to light and, with them, the wrecks of at least 28 vessels. The vestiges of the port facilities of the Etruscan city have been identified in the southernmost part of the excavated area. Subsequently silted up, they consisted of a palisade that acted as a breakwater flanked by a quay built of large blocks of stone. About 6½ feet wide and 52½ feet long, it was connected to a quadrangular structure that jutted outward. Some of the finds associated with these structures (impasto pots, a cup with a graffito inscription in Etruscan, black-glaze vases, an Etruscan column krater) date from as early as the fifth century BC. But the most exciting discovery was that of the 28 boats, together with their cargoes and stores, still in an excellent state of preservation thanks to the wet and anaerobic soil that has prevented deterioration of the timbers and organic substances. The hulls of three cargo boats, three craft for river navigation, an oared ship and two more large vessels whose use has still to be determined are more or less intact, while other hulls are incomplete and damaged. The dates of the ships cover a long lapse of time, extending from the third century BC to the fifth AD, and they must have sunk in the harbor for a variety of motives, ranging from bad weather to human action. The recovery of the material is still underway, as is its restoration, which is going to take a fairly long time. However, some of the objects have already been put on show at temporary exhibitions held in the *Arsenali dei Cavalieri di Santo Stefano.*

Tumulus of Via San Jacopo, eighth-seventh centuries BC. Pisa.

A section of planking, still being excavated, of one of the Roman vessels found at San Rossore near Pisa.

VERSILIA AND THE LUCCA REGION

The port of Pisa was not the only one built by the Etruscans on the coast. One of the more significant of those identified by excavations must have been the port at San Rocchino, in the vicinity of Massarosa, whose faint traces on the ground have now faded. The most significant pieces from this site are now on display in the archeological section of the *Museo di Villa Guinigi* in Lucca, while other objects can be seen at the archeological museum of Viareggio. Other vestiges from the period are present further inland, in Garfagnana, in the valley of the Serchio river and around the ancient lake of Bientina. The materials from these sites are displayed in the archeological museums of Castelnuovo Garfagnana, Barga and Pietrasanta. The Villanovan, Orientalizing and Archaic materials from the settlement at Chiarone di Capannori have gone to the Museo di Villa Guinigi in Lucca, along with some of the

finds from Buca di Castelvenere. Above all, however, the museum houses elegant gold work and the fine Attic red-figure krater with Theseus, the work of the "Painter of the Pig," that was used as a cinerary urn for an Etruscan grave at Rio Ralletta di Capannori; the trove of silver coins from the beginning of the third century BC from Romito di Pozzuolo; the contemporary Ligurian chest tombs from Vado di Camaiore, evidence for the presence of Ligurians in this period; and the chest tomb from Pulica in Lunigiana (third century BC).

Above: small votive bronzes representing women, from Buca di Castelvenere, 450-420 BC. Museo Nazionale di Villa Guinigi, Lucca.

Bowl and dipper, from Chiarone di Capannori, late seventh century BC. Museo Nazionale di Villa Guinigi, Lucca.

Opposite: face of the Attic kelebe attributed to the Painter of the Hog, from Rio Ralletta near Capannori, circa 470 BC. Museo Nazionale di Villa Guinigi, Lucca.

MASSACIUCCOLI LAKE AND THE APUAN MOUNTAINS

The archeological area of Massaciuccoli, facing the lake of the same name, also refers to the Roman era. Open to the public, it contains the remains of a large villa built on terraces at the beginning of the first century AD for the Venulei family of Pisa. While the upper part of the ancient complex is now occupied by the parish church of San Lorenzo, the lower terraces with nymphaea, pools, baths and a triclinium with an exedra can still be seen. Further north, at Capezzano Pianore, a Roman farm with equipment for the production of oil has been brought to light. The materials found on the site are displayed in the archeological museum of Camaiore, while there are plans to open the site of the villa to the public. The oldest marble quarries in the Apuan Alps, dating from the first century BC, were of great importance in the Roman era. Traces of them have been identified through excavation in the environs of Colonnata, Torano and Miseglia. The *Museo Civico del Marmo* in Carrara houses artifacts, coins and religious statues, as well as semifinished materials. Also on display in the museum in Carrara are sections of the surface of ancient quarries, called "slices," that show the marks left by the Roman quarrymen. Other Roman finds are exhibited at the *Accademia di Belle Arti* in Carrara, which can be visited in conjunction with the archeological museum and the excavated area of the ancient city of Luni in Liguria, in the vicinity of Sarzana, a city and port founded by the Romans (177 BC).

Following pages: remains of the Roman villa of the Venulei, first century AD, near Massaciuccoli Lake.

BOLOGNA

The capital of Emilia, located in the heart of a territory inhabited since prehistoric times, was occupied in the ninth century BC by peoples of Villanovan culture from a number of nearby settlements: some of the most important were those of Benacci-Caprara, Benacci, Certosa, Arnoaldi and De Luca. In the first half of the eighth century BC the settlements in the area near Bologna shifted to the west, and the contents of tombs began to grow richer, attaining conspicuous levels between the second half of the eighth century and the first half of the seventh. Further evidence for the flourishing state of the various settlements near Bologna is provided by the store of bronzes found at San Francesco, which originally consisted of a hut housing a partially buried large clay dolium containing about 15,000 objects made of bronze and just three of iron.

Situla della Certosa, last sixth century BC. Museo Civico, Bologna.

Following pages: *Zannoni Stone*, from Bologna, late seventh century BC and the *Benacci Askos*, second half of the eighth century BC. Museo Civico Archeologico, Bologna.

VERUCCHIO

The settlement of Verucchio dates to the period between the ninth and seventh centuries BC. While traces of the inhabited areas have been found in the form of foundations of huts, wells and pottery kilns, it is the tombs that have yielded really spectacular contents. Some of them have even been spared the attentions of looters and the effects of environmental factors. In fact the dampness of the ground and the infiltration of water have preserved materials like cloth, wood, hide, fleece, wicker and food, by protecting them from the action of bacteria. The objects found in Lippi Tomb 85 included wooden objects such as a decorated throne with a high back, a footrest and three round, three-legged tables. Tomb 89, structurally similar, also contained a wooden throne with carvings of scenes from daily life and ceremonial parades. In addition to numerous objects in bronze, including shields made of sheet metal, there was a helmet that still had part of its double crest of horsehair and an ax with its original wooden handle. These materials are on display at the archeological museum of Verucchio.

MARZABOTTO

The fortune of cities like Bologna rose in the fifth century BC, when the loss of Etruscan naval supremacy, after the defeat at Cumae, made the centers on the roads uniting Etruria with the new markets on the Adriatic coast even more important. Marzabotto was built on one of these routes, to the south of Bologna. The city was laid out in a grid on a plateau delimited by a bend in the Reno, its alignment determined by the temples of the acropolis (facing south for religious reasons, and located on the northern decumanus), with a paved cardo and three 50-foot wide decumani. The characteristics of this settlement were determined primarily by religious requirements, as was typical of Etruscan society, and were prior to the principles laid down by Hippodamus of Miletus, the Greek theorist of city planning. The insulae, i.e. the blocks, of Marzabotto were made up of large houses built of unfired brick on a foundation of stones, usually with just one story and workshops and stores facing onto the street. The central entrance led into the courtyard in the impluvium (whose introduction is attributed by literature to the Etruscans), around which the rooms of the house were arranged.

Altar-enclosure D on the acropolis of Marzabotto, early fifth century BC.

Following pages:
Foundations of the south area of Marzabotto, early fifth century BC.

SPINA AND ADRIA

Spina, built at the mouth of a branch of the Po River, was present from the mid-sixth century BC onward, when it became a great trading center where huge amounts of pottery arrived from Attica, later recovered from tombs and displayed at the national archeological museum in Ferrara. The built-up area was divided into several blocks, the largest of which covered 15 acres. The sides exposed to the sea were protected by dikes of pile work, while the blocks – made up of houses with walls of wooden planks or lathwork covered with clay – were separated by a grid of streets and canals. The tombs, found in the areas of Valle Pega and Valle Trebba, were usually simple pits in the ground holding wooden chests. During the fifth century, with the establishment of Syracusan dominance over the Tyrrhenian, Spina's economy was given a new boost as it took on the role of clearing center for the products of its own internal areas and of Central Europe (grain, agricultural produce, timber, metals, amber) on their way to the Greek world. The history of Adria, situated between the Po and the Adige and linked to the sea by a navigable river branch, was similar. Inhabited since the sixth century, and perhaps home to a colony of Greeks, it was eclipsed around the middle of the fifth century by the rise of Spina. In addition to parts of the built-up area, here too formed of wooden houses, various necropolises have been identified.

End of candlestick with crotal player, from Tomb 128 of the necropolis of Valle Trebba at Spina, first-second quarter of the fifth century BC. Museo Archeologico, Ferrara.

All illustrations in this publication have been provided
by SCALA ARCHIVES, the most important source in
the world for color photographs and digital images
of the visual arts.

Over 200,000 subjects are availabe for fast and
accurate iconographic research, at all levels, in the
online database.
www.scalarchives.com

e-mail: archivio@scalarchives.com

© 2007 SCALA Group S.p.A., Florence
All rights reserved
Translation: Huw Evans
Maps: Elia Menigagli

© Photographs: SCALA Group Photographic Archives,
Florence
23a (British Museum HIP\Scala), 113
(Soprintendenza per i Beni Archeologici della
Toscana), 122, 124 (M. Martinelli)

Illustrations, selected from the Scala Archives, of
property belonging to the Italian Republic are
published by concession of the competent authority
(Ministero per i Beni e le Attività Culturali).

ISBN: 978-88-8117-240-5

Printed by: Grafiche Flaminia, Foligno (PG), 2011